MAJOR

MISCONDUCT

MAJOR MISCONDUCT

THE HUMAN COST
OF FIGHTING IN HOCKEY

JEREMY ALLINGHAM

ARSENAL PULP PRESS
VANCOUVER

ARSENAL PULP PRESS
Suite 202 – 211 East Georgia St.
Vancouver, BC V6A 1Z6
Canada
arsenalpulp.com

The publisher gratefully acknowledges the support of the Canada Council for the Arts and the British Columbia Arts Council for its publishing program, and the Government of Canada, and the Government of British Columbia (through the Book Publishing Tax Credit Program), for its publishing activities.

Arsenal Pulp Press acknowledges the xʷməθkʷəy̓əm (Musqueam), Sḵwx̱wú7mesh (Squamish), and səl̓ilwətaʔɬ (Tsleil-Waututh) Nations, speakers of Hul'q'umi'num'/Halq'eméylem/hən̓q̓əmin̓əm̓ and custodians of the traditional, ancestral, and unceded territories where our office is located. We pay respect to their histories, traditions, and continuous living cultures and commit to accountability, respectful relations, and friendship.

The following interviews were developed for CBC's audio series "Major Misconduct: Why We Let Kids Fight on Ice" and are provided courtesy of the CBC: Ryan Diaz, Richard Doerksen, Eric Gottardi, Bruce Hamilton, Georges Laraque, John Ludvig, James McEwan 1, James McEwan 2, Riley McKay, Kaid Oliver, Stephen Peat 1, Stephen Peat 2, Walter Peat, Tim Preston, Jim Thomson, and Naznin Virji-Babul 1.

Cover and text design by Oliver McPartlin
Cover image: Mitchell Layton/National Hockey League via Getty Images
Edited by Shirarose Wilensky
Proofread by Alison Strobel

Printed and bound in Canada

Library and Archives Canada Cataloguing in Publication:
Title: Major misconduct : the human cost of fighting in hockey / Jeremy Allingham.
Names: Allingham, Jeremy, 1982– author.
Identifiers: Canadiana (print) 20190125101 | Canadiana (ebook) 2019012511X | ISBN 9781551527710 (softcover) | ISBN 9781551527727 (HTML)
Subjects: LCSH: Hockey—North America. | LCSH: Sports injuries—North America—Psychological aspects. | LCSH: Violence in sports—Social aspects—North America. | LCSH: Hockey players—North America—Biography.
Classification: LCC GV847 .A45 2019 | DDC 796.962—dc23

For James McEwan, Stephen Peat, and Dale Purinton.
May the strength and courage it took to share these important
stories make hockey a better, safer game.

CONTENTS

FOREWORD

I LOVE the game of hockey! Like most kids growing up in small-town Canada (King City, Ontario), I began skating at the age of four—once you can walk, you can skate. I was drawn to the game because of the speed, competition, physicality, and unity within the team structure. But from as early as I can remember, we were hitting each other on the ice. When I watched *Hockey Night in Canada*, famous commentators Don Cherry and Ron MacLean highlighted and honoured big hits and fights the most. Don Cherry's *Rock 'Em Sock 'Em* videos were a constant Christmas gift, showcasing the best goals, saves, and bloopers but placing the biggest emphasis on the hitting and the fighting. Looking back on my career and life, I can now see that I was trained from a young age to play the game of hockey with the goal of taking away my opponent's will to play. You lean on your opponent through physical force, until they hesitate to go for the puck.

Because of Don Cherry and his videos, kids like me were sitting at home in front of the TV subconsciously absorbing a narrative that self-sacrifice for the good of the team is necessary for the group to succeed. That hate and rivalries are more important than scoring more goals than the other team. That fighting and physical contact are integral components of the sport of hockey.

My path to the National Hockey League (NHL) was not a conventional one. I didn't have any grandiose dreams of one day playing in the NHL. Rather, I was drawn to the game because it was an emotional release for me. Despite the sexual, physical, and verbal abuse I endured during my rookie season in the Ontario Hockey League, I was a thirty-goal scorer, and I had less than a handful of fights over three years. I was not an enforcer yet, but I played the game hard, and I was always the lead, or close, in hits per game. After I was drafted by the Pittsburgh Penguins in 2003, I knew that if I was going to be playing my brand of hockey against grown men, I would have to learn how to defend myself. You see, in hockey, you cannot deliver a clean hit on an opponent without someone else challenging you to a fight. So, in 2005–06, when I was old enough to turn pro and play in the American Hockey League, I gained twenty pounds of muscle in the off-season and began my mission to be the most complete hockey player I could be. And that included fighting.

My first professional fight was against Kevin Colley, a known enforcer and tough customer. I knocked him out. When I got back into the room during intermission, I remember my captain, Alain Nasreddine, looked at me and said, "What the fuck was that?!" I had been to three training camps with Alain, and he knew me as a hockey player, not an enforcer. But my thinking was this: *If I can add enforcer to my resumé, that will get me to the NHL quicker and help me stay around longer.*

Little did I know I would eventually be pigeonholed into a role that would nearly kill me, and rob me of much of the joy of playing hockey at the professional level. I can now see how the subconscious messages I received as a child right through my teens about how to nobly play the game of hockey, combined with the abusive events of my rookie season, shaped me into the reckless, angry, and highly volatile hockey player who was willing to sacrifice himself for the good of the team. This mindset was both my best weapon and my biggest flaw.

Playing the enforcer role took its toll on me physically, mentally, and emotionally. I was nicknamed "Car Bomb" when I was in Philadelphia because of my unpredictable playing style. The fans loved it, but the anxiety I felt when looking at my opponent's lineup during morning skate, knowing that a fight was coming, was difficult to deal with. I had to ignore those thoughts and feelings because they didn't serve me in the enforcer role, but that constant level of stress, and the way I was coping with it, were not sustainable.

By twenty-five, I was in a rehab facility for my dependence on opiates after undergoing two major surgeries in fourteen days. In rehab, I was introduced to spirituality, and it saved my life. It also changed the way I played the game, because I had healed past traumas and gotten to know myself on a deeper level. I knew what my faults were, what my triggers were, and what I needed to do to live a happier and more fulfilling life. I was less angry and emotional, and that equilibrium transferred onto the ice. I was a better teammate and began to fight less. I was lucky enough to go to the Stanley Cup Finals four times with three different teams in my last five seasons. I attribute that success to living the right way and being more aware and conscious of myself and others.

But it wasn't all fun and games.

I have had many diagnosed concussions, my last two from fights and punches to the left side of my head, with no helmet on. The symptoms of my traumatic brain injuries (TBIs) included insomnia, loss of appetite, anxiety, depression, suicidal ideation, head pressure, headaches, impaired vision, light sensitivity, difficulty problem solving, and concentration and impulse control issues.

The final year of my hockey career was an absolute roller coaster. The 2014–15 season began in October; my son was born in November; my best friend, Steve Montador, passed away at the age of thirty-five in February; I received my seventh diagnosed concussion in March; we won the Stanley Cup in June; I decided to retire because of post-concussion syndrome in September; and my grandfather passed away in October. I fell into a deep depression, and I was an unreachable, lost soul for seven months.

When I retired, I was spiritually, mentally, and physically dead. Losing the hockey community, part of my identity, my purpose, and loved ones in such a short period of time, all while suffering the effects of repetitive head trauma, was overwhelming. The mental health complications associated with brain injuries took me to a hell that I want others to avoid, if at all possible. That is why I advocate so passionately for proper understanding, diagnosis, and care for TBIs. That is why I advocate for individuals to continue to seek out different types of treatment for post-concussion syndrome, because without hope and the possibility of a solution, the voices of suicidal ideation can become overpowering. That is what happened to me and what ultimately pushed me into treatment facilities all over the United States and Canada, into reading medical literature, and into spending more than six figures in the past three years in the search to improve my quality of life.

It is my belief that fighting has no place in today's game. Hockey does not need to be sold on hate and rivalries anymore. I believe that the younger generation wants to see skill and speed over violence and hate. The public is now more aware than ever of the risks that athletes are taking for their entertainment. I believe that the NHL and the NHL Players' Association (NHLPA) have to do more to protect their athletes as it relates to concussion protocol, proper diagnosis, and care for traumatic brain injuries. Once the NHL and NHLPA begin to educate the players about the risks of repetitive head trauma, they will not want to bare-knuckle box on ice any longer.

I am against fighting in hockey because of my personal experience. And I will continue to speak my truth about my daily mental health struggles in hopes of reaching as many people and communities as I can, and awakening people to the signs and symptoms of post-concussion syndrome in themselves and loved ones so that they can get help to move into proper diagnosis and care.

I have been on a search for peace. An after reading this book, even though I have yet to meet James, Stephen, or Dale, I feel connected to them. I have experienced the same dark places that they have: hopelessness, a loss of self-identity, impulse control issues, substance abuse, and isolation. The fear of the unknown and what lies ahead is something else that we all seem to share. We are talking about scary issues here. Our brain health will dictate our quality of life moving forward. I hope these young men will find the peace that we are all so desperately seeking.

Books like this are important. They will help educate parents and kids about the risks of playing collision sports. It always comes back to players helping players. I want to thank James, Stephen, and Dale for having the courage to speak about the life-threatening ailments that athletes experience after repetitive head trauma. I hope our stories will save others from experiencing the same suffering and pain that we have. Thank you to Jeremy for putting these stories together. I hope this book serves as a cautionary tale and a vehicle that can drive change in the game of hockey.

Daniel Carcillo
Two-time Stanley Cup champion
Founder of the Chapter 5 Foundation

INTRODUCTION

GROWING UP, my most vivid hockey memory is one that was repeated over the course of countless very early weekday mornings. There I am, standing on skates, in full gear, only barely able to see over the boards. I'm staring out at the lingering fog hovering just above the ice. The rink is cold and quiet. The ice surface is perfectly smooth. It hasn't been touched since the Zamboni's last laps late the night before.

The hour is ungodly (3:57 a.m.) and although it will be only minutes until a parent lets us onto the ice, the moments pass slowly. It feels like an eternity. Every second is excruciating. The anticipation to hit the ice, to mark up that clean sheet with choppy, pint-sized strides, is overwhelming. I just can't wait.

And when that parent comes out, and the gate opens, with its creaking hinges and always-sticky latch, I'm on the loose. The freezing-cold air on my face. The cacophony of steel cutting ice. The echo of wooden sticks on rubber pucks and the near-deafening bass of puck on hollow wooden boards. The whistles. The drills. Bright orange cones zigzagging across the playing surface like on a runway. Our white, smoky breath rhythmically leaving our bodies as our lungs heave for air. We skate, and skate, and skate some more, as the fog lifts to the rafters and the sun rises outside the rink.

It was bliss. It was freedom. It was religion.

Hockey is an easy game to love, and love it is what I've always done.

But there's a dark side of the sport that hides in plain sight. And like a savvy defenseman backpedalling on a dump-and-chase, it interferes with my love for the game.

It's the fighting.

Bare-knuckle boxing on ice has long been accepted and promoted, not only as a necessity in the game but as a promotional draw. "By golly, not only do these men fly across the ice at inhuman speeds, shooting a rubber bullet more than a hundred miles per hour, they also take breaks in the action to pulverize each other's faces!" I can almost hear legendary *Hockey Night in Canada* play-by-play man Bob Cole making the call.

Hockey's history and its current culture are steeped in fighting lore. Go up to pretty much any player or fan and ask them to explain a Gordie Howe hat trick. They'll be quick to tell you: it's a goal, an assist, and a fight in the same game. The inference has always been that a Gordie Howe hat trick is just as good (if not better) than the traditional, and objectively more valuable, three-goal version that brings hats floating down from the crowd like flowers on stage for a virtuoso performance.

And although I'm no fan of fighting now, there was a time when I fully endorsed the scraps. I lived for *Coach's Corner* and *Rock 'Em Sock 'Em* videos. I adored the fighters and chanted "Giiiinnnooo" as number 29, Gino Odjick, patrolled the ice for the Vancouver Canucks at the Pacific Coliseum in the 1990s, ready to punish anyone who dared take a run at superstar Pavel Bure, the beloved Russian Rocket. I even remember publishing a blog as a writer for the mid-2000s hockey reality TV show *Making the Cut* in which I parroted the argument spouted so often by players-turned-analysts: the hockey on the show would be better if the producers and scouts would allow the players to fight for the protection of the stars. And this was no light argument. It was stated as imperative, just as I had heard throughout my childhood from so many intermission panels on *Hockey Night in Canada* and TSN. They *had* to fight, for nothing less than the very safety of the players on the ice. (I believe this kind of argument is known as doublespeak. Like bombing for peace.)

But those pro-fighting feelings changed for me one night at a junior hockey game. The Vancouver Giants of the Western Hockey League (WHL) were set for a Friday night tilt (literally and figuratively) in front of a rowdy hometown crowd at the Pacific Coliseum. Some friends and I had a few beers at our shared East Vancouver house and made our way to the arena. Our buzz was on, the workweek was in the rear-view mirror, and the weekend vibes were good. We settled into our seats about ten rows up and just to the right of centre ice, double-fisting Molsons, talking and laughing loudly, hitting in full stride a quintessentially Canadian night out at the good old hockey game.

All that to say, I wasn't exactly ready for what would become a world view–bending epiphany that fine evening.

Just as the referee released the puck for the opening faceoff, two players dropped the gloves. It was instantaneous. I could've sworn the gloves beat the puck to the ice. Before the game had even begun, there was a fight.

The first thing I noticed was the fans' reflexive bloodlust. The crowd sprang to its feet as one. There was no contemplation and most definitely not a second thought in the building. The reaction was straight from the guts. The Friday night fans were already primed, but this put them right over the top. Ten thousand voices reverberated through the stadium.

The next thing I noticed was the players' faces. Square jaws, for sure, but unmistakably, these were a couple of baby faces. Just kids. We, the crowd, were thousands of fully grown adults (with plenty of kids mixed in) cheering, even demanding, that two children beat the shit out of each other with bare fists on ice.

Haymakers were thrown and received, and after about thirty seconds (which felt more like five minutes), the linesmen stepped in to break it up. The bloodthirsty crowd once again showed its appreciation for the burst of violence with raucous applause.

A fight like this was something, until that point, I would've either celebrated along with everyone else or paid little to no mind. Just a routine donnybrook to set the tone for a big game.

But this time it was different.

I don't know exactly what changed. Maybe it was my own age relative to the players, my proximity to the ice, or the crowd's orchestral, guttural thunder. But one thing I do know is that I felt sick to my stomach.

I borrowed a program from a nearby fan, quickly scanned the roster cards, and found out that the boys who fought were sixteen and seventeen years old. They were children, really. Kids bare-knuckle boxing—for what? For the sake of hockey's fabled "momentum" in the hope of providing early fuel for a team victory? For the players to prove that they're tough enough to make a career in the notoriously violent (and amateur) WHL? To show scouts that maybe, just maybe, they could play and fight at the professional level, and maybe even in the National Hockey League (NHL)? Was it to impress us, the bloodthirsty ticket-buying public?

I had an overwhelming feeling that what I had just witnessed, and implicitly supported, was deeply wrong. I spent most of the rest of the game up on the concourse, drinking a few more beers and trying to forget what had happened and just how foreign my reaction to it had been.

But I couldn't forget. That fight is branded on my brain, even now, more than a decade later. And it left me with so many questions. Questions about our sport, about our culture, and about our values.

Fighting in hockey is a deeply divisive and highly emotional debate that tends to get ugly pretty much as soon as it starts. The level of histrionics and anger that accompany this argument, particularly on the pro-fighting side, has never ceased to amaze me. It is a true powder keg issue that is rivalled only by some of the most toxic conflicts our society has to offer.

My first real experience facing that rage and derision (not to mention the accompanying toxic masculinity and homophobia) came from an innocuous reply I made to a tweet from iconic hockey commentator Don Cherry back in 2013.

Cherry tweeted, with characteristic bombast: "Just saw on one of the tv channels the 5 greatest brawls in basketball. Are ya kiddin me? They were slappin each other."

To which I responded: "@coachscornercbc Fighting in hockey is a disgrace to Canada and the game."

In a matter of minutes, there were dozens of tweets defending Cherry and attempting to smash me (virtually) to smithereens. They ranged from legitimate arguments to personal attacks, and on the extreme end, they were more than a little bit ugly.

There was the boilerplate argument (the one that I, too, had espoused for years) that fighting is intrinsic to hockey, and that I should solve my problem with fighting by not watching, with Shauna @shotzz22 replying: "@jerallingham @coachscornercbc fighting in hockey is & always has been part of the game. If you don't like it change the channel. Easy fix."

My Canadian bona fides were thrown into question by Bakes @bakerbakes_22: "@jerallingham @coachscornercbc if you don't like fighting in hockey, well your adopted and not Canadian #leafsnation #goleafsgo."

And some good old-fashioned expletive-heavy social media name-calling from DJS @dakotajaymes23: "@jerallingham @coachscornercbc fuck you and the horse you rode in on. Get the fuck out."

And then the "mostly all in good fun" category shifted into the reprehensible. First, toxic misogyny from M @pegtrkr: "@jerallingham @coachscornercbc you and your vagina are WRONG! Pussy."

And then, outright homophobia and hatred from eddie hill III @_EH3_: "@jerallingham @coachscornercbc i think ur probably gayer than aids kid."

Without taking up too much space with any more of the responses to my eleven-word tweet opposing fighting in hockey, I was also called, in no particular order: "crybaby," "a disgrace" (multiple), "pussy" (multiple), "tree hugger," "dummy" (multiple), "hipster," "candy ass," "an embarrassment," "idiot," "gun-toting yank" (?), "dumb ass," and "a joke."

Remember what I said about the depth of intensity and anger inherent to this debate?

After the social media circus had subsided, I realized I had hit a nerve and pitched an article about hockey fighting to *Vice*.

On March 6, 2013, a fight between veteran Toronto Maple Leafs enforcer Frazer McLaren and Ottawa Senators rookie Dave Dziurzynski caught the attention of the hockey world. It was Dziurzynski's first NHL fight. It was most certainly not McLaren's. The fight, if you could call it that, happened only twenty seconds into the game. Dziurzynski appeared ready, fists raised in the defensive position, as the players circled each other. But once they engaged, it was clear the rookie was in way over his head. On McLaren's fourth-straight clean shot to the head, Dziurzynski dropped to the ice, face down, arms limp, body still. He was knocked out cold.

A few days later, my article headlined "Fighting in Hockey Is a Disgrace to Canada and the Game" (the very tweet I had sent to Don Cherry) was published by *Vice*. The responses in the comments section and particularly on Facebook made the earlier reactions on

Twitter seem like good-natured ribbing. The hatred, sexism, and homophobia reached disturbing and brutal new lows.

But despite those responses, perhaps even because of them, I was determined to write about fighting in hockey. To have a discussion. To bring the hidden dark side of the game we love into the light.

When I first started investigating fighting in junior hockey for the Canadian Broadcasting Corporation (CBC), I thought I was going to be presenting a debate about one particularly violent part of a sport that is well known to have its fair share of violence. I thought I'd find supporters and detractors of fighting, have a debate, and move on (I was specifically expecting a debate). But what I discovered instead were personal stories. Stories of young men who believed so deeply in their dream of playing pro hockey that they were willing to risk everything—namely, their bodies, and their brains. They may not have known it at the time, but ultimately, they were risking their lives.

What I found in my deep dive into hockey fighting was a cultural force that was shattering lives and leaving the fighters in the dust to pick up the pieces. The fights were bigger than the legend, bigger than the lore. The fights took hold of these young men and changed them irreversibly. And after the fighting was over, they were simply different people. I know the comparison is extreme, but I sincerely believe some of these fighters endure pain and suffering similar to soldiers returning from conflict with post-traumatic stress disorder.

When I write about this subject, it's not only about hockey. It's about the people who play hockey. Those who believe in it. It's about the people who give everything they have to the game and what's left when there's nothing more to give.

Many brilliant books have been written about the hockey fighters whose lives have been lost. This is a book about those who have survived, so far—in some cases, just barely. These men may have played and fought in the professional leagues, but that level of success is fleeting, and for every few years of a hockey enforcer's career, there are often many more to follow filled with pain, uncertainty, and anguish.

When we think of professional hockey players, we most often think of million-dollar contracts, fawning media coverage, and lucrative sponsorship deals. We think of private jets, prime-time TV, and star-struck fans reaching out desperately for autographs. But that life is reserved for the very few who achieve sustained success at the highest level. The vast majority of professional hockey players are blue-collar workers, plying their trade in the minor leagues. They ride the bus. They carry their own gear. In some cases, their paycheques provide barely a living wage. The crowds are modest. The media coverage sparing. It would be hard to argue that the compensation is commensurate with the work, particularly for those fighters who so often face an arduous road to health after their careers are over.

That road includes the fallout from concussions and the possibility of suffering from a degenerative brain disease called chronic traumatic encephalopathy (CTE). The players don't know if they have CTE because the ability to definitively diagnose the disease in living patients is still in development. But what these men do know is that they share painful and dangerous symptoms that are common with the disease. They know they're struggling, and they know something significant has to be done to either stop their lives from spiralling out of control or to save them from certain death.

During my years of research and investigation, I have come to understand that fighting in hockey is a sacred cultural cow. But like all cultural practices left on a pedestal for too long, this one requires further discussion. Further inquiry as to its purpose, and its impact. We must justify this seemingly unjustifiable practice, or let it die.

This discussion might be difficult for some. But it's important that we have a level-headed adult conversation about what is an objectively serious issue that affects the people who pursue our national game. This book examines the lives of regular people who gave themselves to the sport they loved. These men bare-knuckle boxed on ice for a living and now suffer devastating consequences. This is an investigation into the human cost we're willing to tolerate in the name of hockey fighting.

PART 1: JAMES MCEWAN

CHAPTER 1

A DIFFERENT KIND OF FIGHT

McEwan and Boogaard going at it along the near wall. McEwan losing
his helmet already as Boogaard working him over along the glass ...
Mac ducking in right now ... pulls the helmet off Boogaard. Boogaard
caught him early, McEwan hasn't been able to throw a punch.
Boogaard just working him with that right hand. He just knocked him
out right there. I mean, he just caught him flush to the side of the
head and Mac went down.
—James McEwan vs. Aaron Boogaard
(Seattle Thunderbirds vs. Tri-City Americans, October 24, 2004)

THE DARKNESS of the closet was pierced only by the bent light that found its way in. The scant rays flickered and refracted through the relentless tears and danced defiantly across his anguished face. His vision was clouded by agonizing streaks of luminescence. The water from his eyes was warm and salty as it trickled into his mouth. The pain that clouded his brain had taken over his life. It was disorienting. It was often unbearable. And it had to be stopped.

He shook with fear and rage, but he shook too with a yearning. An anticipation. Maybe it was death that would finally bring him the conclusive relief that the drugs and the alcohol only hinted at, a relief he so desperately craved.

As he sat there, rocking on the floor of a rental apartment closet, one question blared across his battered brain like artillery: *What is happening to me?*

It was the summer of death in the hockey world, and in that moment, twenty-four-year-old enforcer James McEwan appeared to be next in line. Rick Rypien, Wade Belak, and Derek Boogaard were all dead, and maybe soon he would be too.

"I just remember sitting in my closet and just crying and being like,

'What's wrong? There's something wrong here,'" McEwan said. "There was multiple times where I definitely had suicidal thoughts. It would overcome me. There was a lot of pain, emotional pain that was like, 'I just want this to stop.'"

In the span of just three months in 2011, three famous and beloved fighters left the world—former Vancouver Canuck Rypien and former Toronto Maple Leaf Belak reportedly dying from suicide, and former New York Ranger Boogaard from drugs.

The deaths shook teammates, coaches, and fans to the core, but to the men across the continent who also made their living bare-knuckle boxing on ice, the demise of their colleagues was so much more. It was a flare, morbidly streaking across the sky, signalling the possibility, perhaps even the likelihood, of their own imminent destruction.

In North Charleston, South Carolina, the foreboding message had been received, loud and clear. McEwan, then a pro hockey fighter with the South Carolina Stingrays of the East Coast Hockey League (ECHL), was deeply concerned that he might share the same fate. "It was this self-destruction that wanted to happen," McEwan recounted. "I see now it was a lot of deep wounds, physically from concussions, and other traumas that were just literally being purged."

Like his hockey-fighting contemporaries, years of bare-knuckle boxing on ice had taken their toll. His body was worn down, but the bumps, bruises, and breaks were nothing compared to what had become of his brain. The headaches were ferocious and unyielding. When they finally relented, they gave way to a fog that was disorienting and debilitating. The anger that broiled within him made his insides feel like a pressure cooker. When released, the emotional outbursts were often violent and uncontrollable. They were as vicious as they were embarrassing, sometimes frightening family and friends just when he needed them most.

And with that kind of all-encompassing pain so often comes self-medication. McEwan drank often and abused Percocet, Tylenol 3s, and morphine pills, the very prescription drugs intended to ease the pain from his career as a hockey fighter. But the temporary relief from the substances proved to be less antidotal and much more cruel, a brief tease at a regular life that, no matter how hard he tried, was at that time out of reach.

McEwan fought often and fought recklessly, like his life depended on it. Although his in-depth training afforded him an abundance of technical skill, his pugilistic style leaned heavily on haymakers and was sometimes a bit thin on defence. It was as though his instinct for self-preservation had faded somewhere along the bumpy path to a minor pro hockey career. Perhaps it never existed in the first place.

He didn't win every time he dropped the gloves, no enforcer does. But the way he fought, someone was guaranteed to lose, and probably lose hard. The destruction wasn't always mutual, but it was most definitely assured. McEwan fought about 200 times throughout his career, and he believes that, beneath the black eyes and the scar tissue, something much more serious was taking place. Like so many of his hockey peers who also trade in violence, McEwan lives with many of the symptoms associated with the degenerative brain disease CTE.

And in that moment, on the floor of a closet, far away from home, those symptoms, and the devastating emotions that accompany them, were pushing him to the brink of suicide.

James McEwan dedicated his life to fighting for his teammates, for his coaches, and for his fans. But now he was fighting for himself. He was fighting to stay alive. Even if just for another few minutes.

"I needed to heal," he said. "I needed to find a way to find peace, to find balance, to reclaim my life, because it was out of control."

James McEwan first hit the ice at the age of four. His earliest hockey memory from that time has nothing to do with sticks or pucks or goals, and it most definitely has nothing to do with fighting. It was mid-game, and while all the other kids were following the puck like a swarm of bees, James was lying out in the middle of the ice, staring at the bright lights on the ceiling. He was making a snow angel. The referee kept telling him to get up, but James wouldn't listen. It was too much fun. Eventually, the man in stripes had to pull him by his arms, along the ice, back to the bench. James was a human Zamboni before he was ever a real-life hockey player.

McEwan grew up in Terrace, a small town of about 14,000 people in northwestern British Columbia, with two younger brothers, his mom, who was a hairdresser, and his dad, who ran the General Motors dealership in town. They lived in a big house that backed onto a big yard with labyrinthine trails twisting through a nearby forest.

Like so many families in so many Canadian towns, hockey was a way of life for the McEwans. Upon closer inspection, you could probably say that James grew up in a quintessential hockey family. He and his brothers, along with their sticks and gear, spent early mornings crammed into the family's Chevy Suburban SUV, pumping each other up, wrestling, arguing, and growing more and more excited as the rink drew nearer.

James always had a competitive edge. It's as if it were programmed into his DNA. He liked to win, and if someone else excelled, he wanted to excel too. The more James played, the more he hungered to get better, faster, and stronger. To skate and pass and score.

Before we move on with James's story, let's be clear about something. No young hockey player ever plans to be a fighter. In their minds they're all Gretzkys and Crosbys and McDavids, scoring that imaginary Game 7 overtime goal and hoisting the Stanley Cup high above their heads as the crowd roars adoringly. Theirs is the classic hockey fantasy that's been repeated for generations on the streets and ponds and rinks of North America.

But for the vast majority of those dreamers, that joyous but naive hockey fantasy ends when the cold reality of talent and competition takes hold of the game. And that's without mentioning the calculated callousness of the business side.

Now, it would be ridiculous to suggest that a kid as young as six could foretell his destiny as a hockey fighter, but for McEwan, that was when the idea of fighting first entered his consciousness, planted like a seed, only to germinate much later. Well, perhaps that's not quite right. The idea of fighting was certainly sown like a seed, but it blossomed more like a land mine.

As James remembers it, bare-knuckle boxing on ice was much less a passive discovery as it was a full-throttle, nineties-techno-fuelled exhortation from a boisterous old man wearing a ruby-red trench coat over a three-piece suit, wraparound shades, and a black fedora.

It was Christmas 1993, and one of James's uncles had found Don Cherry's *Rock 'Em Sock 'Em 5* wrapped with a bow and waiting underneath the Christmas tree. As the tape stammered into the VHS deck, McEwan had no idea that his future, though sanitized and glamorized, was about to be laid starkly before him in all of its graphically violent glory.

"I remember my young nervous system being totally stimulated as I was absorbing it all," said McEwan. "There were grown adult men on the ice punching each other in the face as hard as they could. There was music, blood, and thousands of fans cheering."

And it wasn't just the images. One of Cherry's most famous slogans resonated inside McEwans's head like a gong: "You see, kids, two good guys goin' at it and nobody gets hurt," Cherry bellowed with his trademark bluster.

There's no way that overstimulated six-year-old in Terrace, BC, could've known it, but his acceptance of fighting as an essential part of the Canadian game, and his belief in Cherry's objectively false catchphrase, would later lead him down a dark and dangerous path.

"It was just a part of my life that, I guess, found me," McEwan said. "It was in my karma. It was something I knew that was there, so I went with it."

Fast-forward eight years and fourteen-year-old James McEwan (now living in Kelowna in south central BC) was the pursuit of the Canadian dream personified. The goal of playing pro hockey had become an undying and defining force in his life. And it was then, while barely a teenager, that James first came face-to-face with the stark reality of hockey violence.

In minor hockey, bare-fisted, helmets-off fighting is a rarity, but this particular incident was the exception to the rule. McEwan remembers one of his teammates taking a big hit. James responded promptly by delivering a two-handed slash to the perpetrator with his stick. Before he knew it, James was lying flat on the ice, being schooled in the fundamental system of escalating hockey retribution. Fists were flying. And it didn't feel so good. In fact, it was devastating.

"All of a sudden, my helmet was off, and I got hit with I don't know how many punches before it was over," McEwan said. "I got off the ice and had probably about seven stitches or so above my eye."

That first on-ice assault precipitated an epiphany for James. He always knew that the rough stuff would be part of the game as he grew older, but the severity of the attack, and the injuries he suffered, made self-protection an immediate necessity.

The answer to his problem was obvious. Like so many young players with big-time hockey aspirations, he took up boxing.

"That made me inspired to do boxing more," McEwan said. "I had a coach and worked many years with him and developed it into an art and became pretty good at it, and it transferred over on the ice as well."

Two years later, at sixteen, McEwan was dedicating pretty much all of his waking energy to the hockey dream. But there was just one crucial catch. Compared to most elite players his age vying for a limited number of spots on junior hockey rosters, James didn't have much flash. He was a solid skater with a great feel for the game, but nothing about his skill set really set him apart. It was more his heart, grit, and desire, those apparently vital intangibles institutionalized by the Don Cherrys of the hockey world, that kept his dream alive.

McEwan's junior hockey journey began with disappointment. He was cut by the Trail Smoke Eaters of the British Columbia Hockey League (BCHL). James was down but not out. As he drove to the next tryout with the Merritt Centennials (of the same league), his dream-fuelled pragmatism went into overdrive, quashing any lingering trepidation. He was hell-bent on making the team and couldn't afford to have the scouts ignore him like they did in Trail. This time would be different. This time he'd force them to pay attention with a burst of on-ice violence.

"I just knew. I said, 'I've gotta do something to stand out,'" McEwan remembered. "There was a bigger guy, a veteran guy ... he cross-checked me and I kind of went flying, so I got up and I challenged him. He's a twenty-year-old, I was sixteen at the time, so we squared up and we went toe to toe for a while. It was good. It got a lot of attention."

James had made one hell of an impression. With that fight, he solidified his reputation as a hockey fighter. The punches he took and threw in Merritt were the first of thousands that would help him make teams, win fans, and build a career. Land mine activated.

"I love the expression of that warrior spirit that's in the fighter," said McEwan. "Like the *Rocky* movies, where it's like facing fear, overcoming adversity. It always did something inside of me. From being pretty young, I faced some bullying and got in some fights at school. Looking back at it now, I see it really was an expression of courage, of freedom. There's that surrender. It's like letting go, like bungee jumping. It's like this freedom. [Fighting] was like a drug, and I was addicted to it."

James left Merritt to pursue a tryout with the Prince Albert Raiders of the WHL. He didn't crack the roster (no big surprise—sixteen-year-olds rarely make WHL teams), so he returned to BC from Saskatchewan to play for the junior B Castlegar Rebels of the Kootenay International Junior Hockey League. That season he racked up 420 penalty minutes (PIM), which was among the highest totals in league history.

James's relentless ambition, and fists, meant he wasn't long for the junior B ranks. For any young player consumed with pro hockey dreams, the next big step is often major junior. The following season, James cracked the roster for the Seattle Thunderbirds of the WHL.

The WHL's reputation as a violent league is well established in the hockey world. Former players, coaches, and owners will tell you that, back in the 1970s, '80s, and '90s, full-blown line brawls were not only regular occurrences but simply considered part of the game. Ron Toigo, owner of the Vancouver Giants, told me he remembers a line brawl breaking out every week when he came into the league as owner of Washington State's Tri-City Americans in the early 1990s.

And the ultra-violence from "back in the day" (that persists today, though to a lesser extent) isn't just tolerated; it's celebrated. The on-ice poundings and chaotic scraps are remembered with a fondness usually reserved for precious childhood memories. Fans and former players often tell stories about 1970s New Westminster Bruins coach Ernie "Punch" McLean and his decidedly violent approach to the game with a sweet glimmer of nostalgia in their eyes. And if you want a short synopsis of those stories, just think about some of your favourite scenes from the movie *Slap Shot*, only the blood and teeth littering the ice are real.

Simply put, fighting is in the WHL's lineage, and it's lingered across generations like a dominant gene. Even today, as most leagues, including the NHL, have significantly stiffened the punishments for fighting, the WHL's rules remain some of the most permissive in all of hockey.

For those reasons, "the Dub," as it's affectionately (and sometimes not so affectionately) known, was the perfect breeding ground for James McEwan and his burgeoning career as a hockey enforcer.

In his first two seasons with the Seattle Thunderbirds, McEwan racked up 245 penalty minutes in just 103 games. Before his third season, he was released by the Thunderbirds but bounced back in a major way, fulfilling a long-time goal in the process, by being picked up by his hometown Kelowna Rockets on a tryout. In that following season, McEwan fought more than ever before, accumulating nearly as many penalty minutes as he had in the two previous years combined. With 202 PIM in sixty-eight games, James joined the Rockets' all-time single-season franchise leaders in the stat category (he is still sixth all time), and in the process became a beloved player within the organization and a fan favourite to boot.

It was a lot of fighting. But it paid off for McEwan's career in a big way. (And make no mistake, it was the fighting making the difference. He scored only seventeen points in 208 career WHL games.) Before the beginning of his final season in the Dub, at the age of twenty, he was named captain of the Kelowna Rockets. To this day, earning the captaincy is an accomplishment McEwan remembers with great pride.

What once seemed so distant and theoretical was becoming real. A pro hockey career was so close James could taste it. And maybe, just maybe, all the bloodied hands, broken noses, black eyes, and concussions would pay off in the form of a dream come true.

McEwan has always said that his dream was to play professional hockey. But let's just be clear for a minute. When he, or anyone else, says that, what they really mean is that their goal is to play in the NHL. To compete with the very best in the world. To make the big bucks and skate in front of thousands of screaming fans. By comparison, playing in the American Hockey League (AHL) and hoisting the Calder Cup would undoubtedly be a big thrill and a great line on a hockey resumé, but it's no "name etched into the Stanley Cup, becoming part of hockey history forever" kind of dream.

When James McEwan hit the pro ranks, things got a lot harder. At the age of twenty-one, he started out with the Phoenix Roadrunners of the ECHL, and true to form, he fought more than at any previous point in his career. He racked up 227 penalty minutes in only fifty-nine games. The non-stop scraps and that seemingly non-existent gene for self-preservation were just enough to get him a call-up to the next level. James got his shot at the AHL that season. But it was short-lived. He played four games with the Worcester Sharks (San Jose's affiliate) in Massachusetts, fought twice, and was sent back down. The next season, he was given a tryout with the Manchester Monarchs of the same league, but sickness prevented him from competing for a roster spot. Even though James strongly believes he would've been a regular in the American league if not for injuries, he would never reach that penultimate level of hockey again.

After he was sent back down to the ECHL, it was more of the same for McEwan, but at this level the fighting was much, much different. He had taken on his fair share of full-grown teenagers in the WHL, but now his opponents were consummate professional men who bare-knuckle boxed on ice for a living. These polished hockey-fighting pros were bigger and stronger; they punched harder and took less mercy.

At this point, the shine was coming off McEwan's pro hockey dream. He was a blue-collar brawler, travelling by bus between non-traditional hockey towns and making poverty-level wages. (James says he made about $500 per week.) It was a far cry from the glamour of that NHL dream.

"It's probably the hardest way to make a living," James said. "You don't realize that when you're young, really. It just starts happening because you have a dream, and you're following your dream. That's how it happened for me. And then all of a sudden, it's like, 'This is my life. This is what it is.'"

As he continued along his journeyman's path, playing for the South Carolina Stingrays (his third ECHL team in four seasons), and as that NHL dream faded into the ether, James's health took a severe turn for the worse. First it was the headaches and dizziness. Then the depression. Then the unbridled rage, the drugs, and the alcohol. And finally, James McEwan found himself on the brink of suicide.

"I was fighting, and I was trying to make things happen, but it was like there was something deeper going on," McEwan said. "Something was wrong. I didn't know really what it was. So I started doing research, and I started looking at 'What are these symptoms?' and I started hearing what CTE is. It started to scare me a little bit."

If James's story were unique, this would be a book solely about one man facing down the symptoms common to a brutal degenerative brain disease and courageously living through them. But the story is so much bigger than that. James is not alone. Across North America, more and more hockey fighters are sharing their stories about what it really means to make a living bare-knuckle boxing on ice.

It's an elite and tiny group of men who know what it's like to bring thousands of people to their feet simply by dropping their gloves and trading blows. They know what it's like to be celebrated alongside the superstars of the game and glorified for the brutal violence they've wrought and endured.

They've also come to know the cruel reality that awaited them after their playing days were over. They abused drugs and alcohol. They stole, they lied, and they committed crimes. They alienated family and friends. They ended up behind bars.

Fighting in hockey is still accepted by many as an important part of the Canadian game and, by extension, an inherent part of the Canadian cultural fabric. By that logic, if hockey fighting is not only acceptable but also inherent to our culture, does that also mean that the long-term suffering of the players who fight is acceptable? Does it mean that the death of hockey enforcers is part of our cultural fabric?

Does it mean that it's acceptable to us that a twenty-four-year-old fighter sits in his closet, considering suicide as his only remaining option to end the pain?

Hockey enforcers like James McEwan spend their lives fighting on ice to protect their teammates and entertain their fans, but when their playing days are over, who's left to fight for them?

The sport of hockey has always been presented as a lifelong pursuit. But for those who sacrifice themselves in the name of a dream, it is much more temporary. And while James McEwan's time as a high-calibre pro prospect was most certainly temporary, the injuries he picked up along the way were not. James had a tough road ahead.

CHAPTER 2
PUNCHING MYSELF IN THE FACE

Emmerson ... pounding away on McEwan. McEwan hangs in there.
And Emmerson back with two uppercuts. Great scrap here! Finally
they both go down! A couple of good warriors there, and both are
okay! McEwan took some big bombs and delivered a couple himself. He
just kept throwing them. Emmerson okay and McEwan okay!
—James McEwan vs. Riley Emmerson
(Seattle Thunderbirds vs. Tri-City Americans, November 20, 2005)

EVEN THOUGH the injuries to James McEwan's brain would leave a legacy of pain and fury for years to come, they weren't the ones that ended his hockey career for good. Even without concussions and CTE, the physical toll hockey fighters are forced to withstand can be described, at minimum, as punishing and, at maximum, as inhuman.

Like the unrelenting hockey warrior he was, McEwan made multiple attempts to return from his surgeries. At one point, he underwent six in five years. He fought through damaged fists, elbows, shoulders, and more (most of which, he says, were a direct result of fighting), only to become reinjured, again and again.

And with those injuries came the continued use and abuse of drugs and alcohol. The first incidents of serious drug use happened during his second season with the Kelowna Rockets when he was twenty. McEwan had been prescribed painkillers after being stepped on by a skate. Long after the injury healed, he'd break the pills out at parties to go with the booze. James used the painkillers more and more, and eventually became addicted.

Two years later, in 2010, after his second year pro, McEwan was playing for the Ontario Reign (based in California) of the ECHL when he was jarred by a couple of tough wake-up calls. The death of a close friend's mother and another death in his own family forced him to reflect in a significant way. James promptly quit drinking and taking prescription drugs and instead started using cannabis to deal with his pain. He continued to use cannabis for a stretch but had a nagging feeling that there was something more out there for him.

As the final couple of years of his hockey dream ran their course, James had a life-altering out-of-body experience. On a podcast hosted by American entertainer Joe Rogan he heard about something called dimethyltryptamine (DMT).

For some reason, whether it was the pain and the surgeries he had been facing, a yearning to experience a deeper reality, or simply a curiosity that was piqued, James felt driven to explore DMT, which he refers to as a medicine. "This was something that my soul told me that I had to do," McEwan said. "I hesitate to share this because of the stigma that comes along with that. I don't want to be put off as 'You're just messed up on drugs.' It wasn't that experience for me. It was a powerful spiritual experience for me. I was waking up, and I feel like the veil of reality was kind of being lifted."

"I ended up coming across a person ... Her friend made it from bark off of Vancouver Island and gave me some," McEwan recounted. "She ended up getting it sent to me, and then I had to figure out how to use it. I wasn't a drug user at the time, so I was like, 'What do I do with this stuff?' There wasn't a lot of information about it at the time."

DMT occurs naturally in the bodies of many plants and animals, and can be inhaled, injected, or ingested. James chose to smoke it. The high only lasted about fifteen minutes, but the depth of the archaeological dig into his psyche was earth shattering. And much like archaeologists tend to do, James was able to find some of the missing pieces of his existence and put them together for a clearer, more complete picture of his world.

"Time dissolved, everything dissolved, and I went into a different dimension," James said. "I was laughing and crying at the same time because I was like, 'Oh my God, I've just been answered.' I wasn't afraid of dying then. My fear of death kind of left. And the truth was just kind of shown to me. When I came back from the experience, I felt like there was this knowing and this understanding of something greater, and knowing that we're all connected and part of something amazing."

So what happens when a man who makes his living fighting has an epiphany about the oneness of humanity and the world, but then still has to go out and scrap? That paradox led to a seminal moment in James's career and in his life. In one of his final pro fights, coincidentally against another former Kelowna Rocket, everything around him slowed down.

"We dropped the gloves, and it was like things went in slow motion," McEwan recalled. "I was punching him and he was punching me, and then it was like this realization where I was punching myself in the face ... The fight stopped, the refs came in, and I started skating to the dressing room. Everything was still slowed down. A lot of fans were drunk and screaming and going crazy. It was like a circus."

McEwan had always been a hockey fighter with a heart of gold, but now he was a hockey fighter who had come to see his trade as a bizarre and self-destructive freak show, performed for alcohol-fuelled and bloodthirsty hordes of screaming fans. Pair that epiphany with the non-stop injuries, and his exit from the game became inevitable.

"I was like, 'This doesn't feel right anymore. This doesn't seem right,'" he said. "It didn't seem in alignment, and it felt really weird. I had a moment where I was like, 'There's a better way.' I just thought there's something better I can do with my energy than punching someone else. I couldn't go back after that. I couldn't go back to the way that things were."

After years of striving, sacrificing, and fighting, it was that slow-motion moment coupled with a laundry list of physical injuries that finally forced McEwan to give up on his pro hockey dreams. There were the broken hands, the severed tendons (that required a tendon transplant), the separated shoulder, a torn rotator cuff, the bad knees, and finally, a broken hip that had left him in a state of disrepair. Dreading the surgery and the painful rehabilitation to follow, and building upon his shifting consciousness, James requested of his ECHL team that he be allowed to return home to Kelowna and heal naturally, without surgery. His request was promptly denied. But James had made up his mind. He left the team and headed for home.

James McEwan finally left hockey behind. He left behind the good and the bad. The goals and the victories, the bruises and the breaks. The teammates and the roaring crowds, the pain and the dread. The childhood memories, the punches to the head.

After that challenging 2011–12 year in South Carolina, McEwan called it quits.

But just because he was finally ready to leave the game, that didn't mean the game, and all of its rippling aftershocks, was ready to leave him. Not by a long shot.

"It's kind of like a hangover," McEwan said. "It's great when you're high, but then the next day can suck. It's not even so much the next day, it's years down the line ... where the accumulation of things started to add up."

James took the next two and a half years to mend. Slowly, through yoga, what he describes as "intense spiritual practices," and physiotherapy, McEwan grew stronger and stronger. He surprised even himself with the speed and fullness of his recovery.

When he first returned home with the hip injury, James was all but certain his hockey career was over. That he was leaving everything behind, including the fights and the injuries. But as he healed and his body proved time and time again that it was ready to go, he started to change his mind. McEwan just couldn't shake the itch. Hockey was the only career he'd ever known, and if this was one last unexpected chance to play the game at a professional level, he was going to take it.

James landed a tryout with the Gwinnett Gladiators of the ECHL, in Georgia, just northeast of Atlanta. James was happy to be back.

But the good vibes surrounding his umpteenth comeback wouldn't last. In an early-season fight, James fell under the weight of his opponent, and his skull whipped back and smashed into the ice. He had suffered yet another serious concussion.

As always, James held out hope and worked relentlessly through multiple months of rehab to make his way back to the ice. This time, it took until the new year. Upon his return, James did what he always did: fight, and fight hard. But his reckless style caught up with him one last time. On this occasion, James took a beating that truly rearranged his face. In his final on-ice bout, he took so many powerful punches that his face became freakishly contorted. It swelled up like a blowfish. His opponent's jack-hammering fists had all but destroyed his face and left him with yet another concussion. It was ugly. And it hurt. Real bad.

That was it. The final comeback had failed. His body was worn down more than ever. His brain had sustained even more damage.

There was no coming back from these final setbacks. James's stats from the final season of his career:

21 games played

0 goals

0 assists

67 penalty minutes

1 major concussion

1 super messed-up face

Most hockey careers end not with a bang but a whimper. As skill, strength, and speed fade, players skate off into the great hockey sunset, never to return. But not James McEwan. His career ended the way it was played, violently and with a loud bang. The bang just so happened to be his face bending and swelling and his brain smashing against the inside of his skull. Unfortunately, James wasn't able to leave a mark on his final game in professional hockey, but, boy, did that final game leave its mark on him.

After leaving Georgia, James's spiritual journey shifted into high gear. It was like turning off a dirt road and heading out onto the autobahn. Just months after hanging up his skates for good, he embarked on a life-changing trip to India. There he met the man he calls his guru and solidified his commitment to divine powers. He immersed himself in meditation and the teachings of Kriya Yoga (an ancient form of yoga that was revived for modern times and brought to the West in the 1920s).

"I surrendered to the divine," McEwan told me. "I let everything go and focused on my connection with God on the spiritual path. That was a big part of my healing."

Upon his return to Kelowna, he settled, however uneasily, back into his life at home. It had been about five years since James had decided there was no more room for alcohol and party drugs in his life. They left him feeling even worse than he usually did and only exacerbated his depression and brain injuries. It was a pretty straightforward decision that millions have made: quit the booze and the drugs, and hope to feel better. It worked for James, but that didn't mean it was always easy.

Any medical professional, or reasonable person, for that matter, would tell you that James opting out of drugs and alcohol was an excellent choice. A no-brainer, really. As someone living with severe mental health issues caused by brain injuries, avoiding intoxicants that are only designed to further cloud the mind seems like a good way to go. But when you've changed, and the place where you once lived hasn't necessarily done the same, the process of re-acclimatizing can be difficult.

At the time, James was a twenty-eight-year-old newly retired hockey player. Most of his friends were either current or former hockey players too. His brothers were hockey players. And for many hockey players, particularly at that age, alcohol (and certainly drugs) are central to social life.

Many people close to James struggled to understand why he had given up on booze and drugs. Giving up on booze was giving up on rowdy Friday nights, on all-night benders, on laughs, on pranks, on shenanigans, on brotherhood. Really, giving up on booze was like giving up on friendship. And, in an alcohol-centric culture, having one friend give up on booze can force others to re-evaluate their own habits, to take a hard look at their own use. That can be a scary thing. Too scary and too real for many.

"A lot of guys in the hockey community have beers all the time, and it was strange for me not to be having alcohol," McEwan said. "And it was also really challenging for me for a little while too because that was my social life ... then I stopped. When someone changes out of the norm you know, it's kind of like, they think that person's weird or they're different now. It can make other people feel uncomfortable because most people know that alcohol isn't healthy."

McEwan had a small group of friends who had his sober back, but what often happens in these situations happened to him too. Instead of serious self-reflection, many of his friends doled out plenty of criticism and even ostracism. And it was that criticism, that ostracism that led to one of the scariest moments of James's experience with brain injuries.

According to James, he and an acquaintance were cruising around Kelowna on their way to a party. At this point, James was off alcohol but still in the social circle. His passenger was needling him for quitting drinking. Why did he have to be so weird? Why couldn't he just enjoy a beer with the boys like everyone else? The criticism had gone beyond friendly ribbing and was getting personal.

James reacted not with a straightforward rebuttal, or even a curt fuck off, but instead, he flew into an uncontrollable hurricane of rage. His hands strangled the steering wheel. He shook with a kinetic and destructive anger. His foot weighed 1,000 pounds, pushing the pedal to the floor and the vehicle to its limits. And as if all that wasn't frightening enough, James's scream was primal. He likened it to the scream of a murder victim.

"There was rage flowing through every cell in my body," McEwan said. "The fury was so intense it made me feel like my eyes were going to burst out of my head."

In that moment, James was once again pushed to the brink of death, but this time, someone else was along for the ride. James says his passenger was terrified, crying and begging him to pull the car over.

Finally, mercifully, he did. But the torrent of rage was unceasing. The dam had burst.

James jumped out of the SUV and slammed the door with every ounce of his strength. Then he did it again. Then again. And again. And again, until the door hung from its hinges. Despite the mammoth physical effort he was exerting, the crying and the screaming continued unabated. McEwan's primordial howling reverberated through the atmosphere like coming war.

Today, James looks back on this incident and others like it and feels thankful. "I am lucky to be alive and even more lucky I didn't kill anyone else in one of these episodes, which are proven to be common symptoms of CTE," he said.

James may have escaped the day-to-day violence of his job as a hockey fighter, but his brain injuries, and all of their ugliness, had followed him home.

CHAPTER 3
THE AYAHUASCA PATH

And here we go ... drop of the puck, pitter patter let's get at 'er! It's gonna be McEwan and Hunt ... They're going to drop the gloves at centre ice. They're going to do a dance of a different kind ... Nice punches from McEwan, another from McEwan! Nice right here that connects! Now a left to the side of the head of Hunt ... another couple of quick shots here by McEwan! Linesman jump in, bing bang boom, right off the hop, three seconds in ... McEwan the victor! What do you say? It's the same old, same old. James McEwan, looks like he's in mid-season form ... I will never grow tired of watching those two guys go!
—James McEwan vs. Garet Hunt
(Kelowna Rockets vs. Vancouver Giants, September 26, 2007)

I WANT you to picture yourself inside an ice rink. The thick air, the stark cold, and the chaotic sounds of skates and pucks and whistles and kids and, of course, the Zamboni. The rink is a cacophony. It's an unknowing symphony.

Now try, if you will, to picture the most opposite possible place to that ice rink. There's a good chance you're thinking of a place that is warm and humid. Someplace natural and wild. It's probably a place that's surrounded by massive trees and exotic flora and fauna. Maybe, just maybe, you're thinking about the Amazon rainforest.

And who could argue with that? The quiet, heavy, humid heat of the Amazon is about as far away as you can get from the freezing-cold chaos of the hockey rink. And that opposite Amazon is crucial to James McEwan's story because it was a traditional spiritual medicine from that very rainforest that he says helped save him from the injuries and illnesses he suffered at the ice rink. Without the Amazon, and the indigenous brew known as ayahuasca that comes from it, James isn't so sure he would still be with us, alive, in the world today.

After his playing days were over, McEwan was looking for almost anything that would improve his situation. Anything that would help him escape the brutal pain he was experiencing. Anything that would help him regain control of the spiral. Ayahuasca was that anything, and so much more.

James was back living in Kelowna. He was no longer a hockey player. He had been off alcohol and drugs for some time. But despite the positive changes he'd undertaken, the depression and the symptoms of his brain injuries were only growing worse. No matter how hard he tried, no matter how desperately he wanted to, he couldn't quell the raging storm inside.

As the depression, the anger, and the suicidal thoughts reached crisis levels, James finally sought medical help. His doctors recognized the problems he was facing and did what most doctors do: prescribed pills. Antidepressants to dull the pain. But although those kinds of pills have worked wonders for many living with mental health issues, James was determined to steer clear. He wanted to find another way.

So he turned to meditation, along with his yoga practice, as a healing spiritual means of addressing his pain. And he took that practice to new levels, at one point attending a ten-day silent meditation (a Vipassana) in the mountains of south central British Columbia.

James also learned about what he calls "sacred plant medicine." "I was searching for everything. I was desperate," McEwan recalled. "I found out about ayahuasca, and I just felt like this is something that could help, and I was listening to what doctors were saying about it and how it was helping people hooked on heroin ... and helping with a lot of people with depression."

If becoming a pro hockey player was the singular focus for the first part of James's life, healing from his brain injuries and finding balance in the chaotic midst of his mental health issues was the equivalent focus for his life after the game. James saw ayahuasca as a perfect and powerful complement to the meditation, spirituality, and healthy living he was already pursuing. And perhaps, he thought, it could even help release him from the grips of depression and suicide.

Ayahuasca is a psychoactive drink usually prepared by shamans or other practitioners to be used in ceremonies where its consumption is treated as a solemn sacrament. Christian missionaries first learned about the plant-based concoction in the sixteenth century. Indigenous South Americans had been using it for centuries before that.

Although its roots are in South America, ayahuasca's growing popularity as a healing compound, and as a tourist experience, means it is now available in North America. But that doesn't mean it's easy to come by. The brew is much harder to find than more common illegal street drugs. According to people who have used ayahuasca, there are many practitioners throughout the United States and Canada who work underground, on a word-of-mouth basis for fear of police reprisal. That's because the psychoactive compound found in ayahuasca, DMT (the hallucinogen McEwan initially experimented with), is an illegal Schedule III drug in Canada and an illegal Schedule I drug in the United States.

A regular dose of ayahuasca will usually take effect about a half hour after consumption, and that's when the psychedelic roller-coaster ride begins. The effects can include visual and auditory hallucinations, as well as intense introspection that can lead to powerful emotions. Ayahuasca is also known to increase the heart rate and blood pressure, and can sometimes cause violent vomiting and diarrhea. Although ayahuasca is generally considered to be safe when consumed with appropriate expert supervision, some recent ayahuasca ceremonies have resulted in the deaths of tourists, and there is no medical consensus on its effectiveness in treating the myriad illnesses it is said to help with.

However, ayahuasca has support from one of the world's foremost experts on addiction. Dr Gabor Maté from Vancouver, BC, has worked with the hallucinogenic substance and taken it himself. He writes that, when used correctly, ayahuasca can put people in touch with their repressed pain and trauma, the very factors that he says drive all dysfunctional behaviours. "Consciously experiencing our primal pain loosens its hold on us," Maté writes. "Thus ayahuasca may achieve in a few sittings what many years of psychotherapy can only aspire to. It may also allow people to re-experience inner qualities [that have] long been missing in action, such as wholeness, trust, love and a sense of possibility. People quite literally remember themselves."[1]

Maté believes that the power of integrating the mind and body, along with the nervous and immune systems, is an idea that is under-appreciated in conventional Western medicine. Maté says he's seen incredible holistic healing, including of a woman who suffered from an often-fatal autoimmune condition. At one point, she was interested in doctor-assisted death, but after working with ayahuasca, Maté says, she felt better and moved around independently. Another case Maté writes about is a patient who attempted suicide a dozen times. Today, he says, that patient is animated by energy and hope. "I have witnessed people overcome addictions to substances, sexual compulsion, and other self-harming behaviours," Maté writes. "Some have found liberation from chronic shame or the mental fog of depression or anxiety."[2]

Indeed, a June 2018 study by researchers out of the Brain Institute at the Federal University of Rio Grande do Norte in Brazil (and published in the journal *Psychological Medicine*) found that ayahuasca acts as an effective rapid antidepressant to address treatment-resistant depression—that is, depression that does not respond to more commonly prescribed remedies. The researchers conducted a parallel-arm, double-blind, randomized, placebo-controlled trial with twenty-nine subjects. They gave patients either a single dose of ayahuasca or a placebo. Depression levels in the ayahuasca patients were, at all times, lower than those in the placebo group. There was even a trend toward significant remission in the ayahuasca subjects. The researchers concluded, "This study brings new evidence supporting the safety and therapeutic value of ayahuasca, dosed within an appropriate setting, to help treat depression."[3]

Through research and interviews, I've discovered that each ayahuasca experience can be very different, but it's the first one that is often the most transformative. I've heard joyous stories of inspiration and deep inner reflection, and I've heard about terrifying moments of trauma and pain unearthed, breaking down walls, like waters bursting through a dam.

Dr Maté says his first experience with an ayahuasca ceremony was beautiful. "I was deeply in touch with love," he said. "I started crying. Tears of love and joy started flowing down my face and I realized what love really was, which wasn't an emotion toward one person, it was actually a state of being. It didn't stay with me ... because you have to integrate it, but I got the power of it, and I also understood why people were asking about it."

During my interview with Dr Maté, I made the mistake, multiple times, of referring to ayahuasca as a therapy. He was quick to point out that it shouldn't be referred to as such, because it's not like a prescription. You don't go home with it, take it a certain number of times, and then you're better. It's part of a larger healing process that, for many people, takes time.

"I don't call it a treatment. It's a ceremony. If you meditated today, might you want to meditate tomorrow again?" Maté asked me.

I replied that you very well might.

"Same as ayahuasca," he continued. "It depends how deep you want to go. Some people do it once, and they say it's fine. Other people are called to do it again. Other people do it repeatedly for years and years and years. It's not as a treatment. It's not like you take the drug home and you drink it every day. It's a certain experience that takes you inside yourself or inside your spirit in a very profound way, and why wouldn't people want to do that?"

Maté said that this particular drug has the power to not only change lives but also to entice people to dedicate themselves to it, almost entirely.

"I know people, like practitioners I've worked with, have done it thousands of times," he said. "But that's their life. That's what they do. If you don't think of it as a treatment, but you think of it as a practice, then it's like yoga or meditation, but you wouldn't stop at a certain point. It could be your path, and for some people it is."

Despite the promise of ayahuasca, Dr Maté warned that it is not a panacea but a plant-based medicine that needs to be treated carefully and respectfully.

As for James McEwan, he says his first experience with ayahuasca was gentle but brought up a lot of fears about the health challenges he was facing and the struggles with his life's purpose. "I was just wanting to heal and connect spiritually," McEwan said. "[I needed] to connect to my purpose and find out who I really was and ask, 'What am I supposed to do in life now?' because my life dissolved because hockey was my whole life for the most part."

James has told me that ayahuasca can often allow people to step away from the self they know and the everyday paradigm they've come to accept as normal. He says it's like looking down on yourself from high in the air, and that 100-metres-up perspective allows for a lot of questioning and evaluation. "The medicine will show you parts of yourself that you might not be aware of," McEwan said. "Because a lot of how we're living is on autopilot to our subconscious programming. So this can kind of pull you back from that and allow you to observe. And sometimes you'll do it and it'll be intense and you'll see the things you want to change and some of the things you've done in your past, and that can be tough to look at sometimes. But that's where the change begins, [with] the awareness of the things that need to be changed."

And much like Dr Maté's first time, a lot of James's ayahuasca experiences have boiled down to an appreciation and understanding of one thing: love. "What I experienced ... is that love is everything," he said. "It's love that is the most important thing because it is everything. Love isn't just an emotion; it's far beyond that. Love is the essence of everything ... pure creation and everything in between."

James used ayahuasca twelve times. These were deep explorations of his psyche and of his soul. It felt good. The symptoms associated with CTE were subsiding. The depression visited less often. The anger was becoming more manageable. James felt like he was getting his life back. "I imagine that the physiological effects of my brain were changing," he said. "When you have a medicine and you know it's helping you, I just dedicated everything to it because nothing else mattered."

But like everything else along James's path, pursuing ayahuasca came with its challenges. Just like when he quit drugs and alcohol, he received pushback from his loved ones, who weren't prepared for the wholesale night-and-day change they saw in him. To put it bluntly, he had become an entirely different person. You can imagine how difficult it must've been for his friends and family to witness a transformation so drastic. One day, you have an all-Canadian hockey kid, pursuing the NHL dream and throwing back a few brewskis with the boys. The next, you have a bearded, turbaned young man dedicating his life to a form of spirituality you're not familiar with and a South American healing drink you can barely pronounce.

But for James, his progress was becoming more and more apparent, so he continued to dive in headlong. "At the time, it was like a fight for my life," McEwan said. "And then to see it working, I knew it was good. Even though a lot of people didn't really understand it because I started changing a lot from being a fighter ... These things that weren't serving me started to dissolve, which ended up bringing a lot more balance, a lot more peace, a lot more happiness in my life."

After the publication of a CBC article I wrote about James, and the revelation that ayahuasca ceremonies have played a big role in his healing and recovery, he says a number of hockey players reached out to him wanting to find out more about taking part in a ceremony. He even heard from a former opponent who said the medicine was working for him too.

Although James is supportive of the idea of more people accessing ayahuasca, much like Dr Maté, he warns that it's not a cure. McEwan thinks it's a tool to be used along with other important actions along the path to recovery. "It's not the be-all, end-all, cure-all," he said. "It's a lifestyle change, and it takes work to undo [brain damage]. It takes daily meditation, it takes eating the right things, it takes doing the practices and doing the work. Ayahuasca's a good tool but maybe not for everybody."

The symptoms associated with CTE were still in his life, but now James had a collection of complementary tools and a clear course of action in the face of impending doom. From that point on, ayahuasca, meditation, and yoga would serve not only as his escape valves but as his life's work. And along with the relief they provided, these passions filled the void and dulled the pain left behind by his recently lapsed hockey dreams.

CHAPTER 4
TRUTH IS MY NAME

This is our friend, James McEwan ... yes it is, McEwan just called up
from Phoenix ... his first American game and he's lookin' to make an
impression here ... and they're both getting in some decent shots!
—James McEwan vs. Matt Clackson
(Worcester Sharks vs. Lehigh Valley Phantoms, January 14, 2009)

I FOUND James McEwan in the Kelowna Rockets' record book. When I searched for him on Facebook, I came across a guitar-playing, turban-wearing dude. He exuded spirituality and self-confidence. At first I thought I had the wrong guy. But once I compared pictures old and new, and realized it was him, I knew he'd have an important story to tell.

McEwan and I exchanged emails and spoke on the phone a couple of times. I was taken with his charisma and his courage to speak about the difficult challenges he had experienced during and after his hockey career. To do the story justice, I knew we'd have to meet, face-to-face.

I had a few hours to think about McEwan and his incredible story as I drove through the snow-kissed peaks of the Coquihalla Highway between Vancouver and Kelowna on a quintessentially crisp BC autumn day. Because my paltry fighting resumé boasts only a couple of youthfully exuberant (and ill-advised) barroom dust-ups, the idea of a high-profile professional life of fighting is hard for me to imagine. We've all seen the fights live at the rink or on *Hockey Night in Canada*, but to do it yourself, consistently over the course of a season, or many seasons, and sometimes on demand, strikes me as an intellectual and physical leap too far.

And however foreign the concept of bare-knuckle boxing on ice professionally might be, the idea of abandoning that fighting life and committing to something so perfectly and spiritually opposite like ayahuasca and yoga is maybe even harder to digest.

How is it possible for a person to transform so thoroughly? How can you spend years devoted to violence in the realm of sport, only to then devote yourself to a centuries-old spiritual tradition focused on awakening the peace that exists deep within your soul?

I wonder if the best way to explain it is to say that, at the age of thirty-one, and under intense existential pressure, McEwan has changed his life as drastically as one can. Or is it only fair to say that these are two distinct lives lived by the same person but not necessarily within the scope of a shared consciousness? Perhaps that shared consciousness exists, but if it does, the remaining connection between those lives must be threadbare.

With a firestorm of existential questions guiding my drive, I headed into Kelowna, where James and I were set to meet at an independent tea shop of his choosing. I pulled my work vehicle up to the side of the road, and within a couple of minutes, McEwan emerged from a blue Honda Civic.

If all you'd ever heard about James McEwan was that he was a fierce hockey fighter who took on some of the toughest players on skates for a living, you'd probably be surprised by his appearance. You might even straight-up refuse to believe it was him. Knowing well what James looked like from social media, I wasn't surprised so much by his look—jeans and a black jacket, accented by a long beard and white cotton turban (customary garb for a practitioner of kundalini yoga)—as I was by his air. There was a calmness you might expect from a yoga practitioner and musician, but also an unexpected cautiousness.

I'm fully aware that some of McEwan's caution had to do with meeting an unknown reporter who had seemingly picked him out of nowhere and contacted him through social media for a CBC Radio documentary about fighting in junior hockey. But it was more than that. Through the process of getting to know James, I've understood that he's highly perceptive and knows that even though he believes deeply in the life he's chosen, and pursues that life with an intense discipline and commitment, not everyone gets it. Some people think it's a bit weird and flaky. That realistic self-perception of his current life is only exacerbated by having spent so much time in the monoculture that is the hockey world. It is overwhelmingly white, male, heterosexual, cis, and often comes with a strong dose of toxic masculinity. The machismo. The tough-guy facade. The complete rejection of vulnerability. In hockey there's a set way of being and seldom room for anything different.

As we settled into the café's plush furniture, with the soothing aroma of our teas filling the air, James and I had a telling exchange before the official conversation.

He spoke deliberately and directly, asking me: "What is your intention with my story?"

I was a bit thrown off by the question. As a CBC Radio journalist, I'm usually under intense deadline pressures, working on multiple stories at once and rushing to deliver clips that might be as short as thirty seconds. There's rarely time to slow down and take a measured macro look at what I'm doing, let alone what I intend to do. Usually, I just do. It's that simple.

But as James and I discussed our vision further, and the initial tension of meeting released, I realized not only that this was a trust-building exercise, but more broadly, that this was simply how James lived his life now, with careful consideration, deep thought, and calculated purpose.

James and I watched videos of some of his most explosive on-ice brawls. His memory of fights that happened more than a decade ago was impressive. It was as though the buildup and the nerves, followed by the adrenaline, the violence, and the letting-go, had branded those moments onto his brain forever. The way he so vividly and immediately recalled them, it was almost as though those violent encounters had left their own particular kind of indelible neural pathway.

Because what James did was so difficult, and has historically been carried out by such a small celebrated group, at that point he was still proud of what he had accomplished with his fists. The feeling remained strong, despite the life-altering injuries he had suffered. But there was a distance from it all too. He tended to refer to that previous James who fought for a living as decidedly other, sometimes even using the third person. After a lengthy silence, he reflected upon one of the scraps we watched. "There's a feeling of ... reverence, of honour, for both guys," he said. "Both those guys were out there, and they put their heart and soul into that, and you know you have people looking up to you. You have fans, you have family. So there, I see two warrior spirits out there expressing that the best way they can."

Some of the most intense moments in the first hours of getting to know James McEwan happened when I asked highly personal questions about his brushes with death. I inquired about his experiences feeling compelled to die. To take his own life and leave everything behind. And although it may seem like a topic of conversation inappropriate for two people who had just met, I didn't feel uncomfortable. James's aura was calm and welcoming.

As a journalist, I've come to learn that when someone, like James, is prepared to be open and vulnerable, it can lead to moments and stories that are beautiful in their directness and powerful in their universality. The anticipated awkwardness never materializes, because nothing could be more real, with less pretense and clutter, than an open discussion about a life-and-death decision.

When I first asked James about suicide, he took a long pause. This was less his trademark cautiousness and more an emotional gathering within himself. His voice grew softer and trembled. And then, memories of harrowing moments flowed forth. "There was multiple times where I definitely had suicidal thoughts," McEwan said. "It would overcome me, and ... there was a lot of pain. It was like emotional pain that is like, 'I just want this to stop. I want this to stop.' So yeah, there's been times where there's literally been a knife to my wrist, and just, 'What am I doing?' That pain was running rapid ... it was like this self-destruction that wanted to happen. It was trying to take me over. It was really intense."

We took the time to explore those life-altering moments, and when James was done, the next question became obvious. When he found himself in those abject, desperate moments on the brink of death, how did he survive? How did he stay alive when forces within him were pushing, and demanding, that he make the pain stop once and for all?

"I feel like there was just a little bit of space," James recalled. "I would see the devastation from other suicides and how I had a friend who was on a hockey team and he committed suicide. There was something in me that was like, 'No, you're not going to do this.' It was kind of like the angel and the devil on the shoulder. It's like, 'Which one are you going to buy into right now?' There was that little bit of space ... I guess that's the best way to put it."

At that, James took a well-deserved break from remembering, in detail, some of the lowest points of his life. We took a picturesque walk beside Okanagan Lake, continuing our conversation and preparing for the next item on the docket: a visit to a kundalini yoga class that McEwan himself would be leading.

Pulsating hand drums. An unbroken, surging bass synth. Pings of a vajra bell. And the beautiful, melodic repetitions of a sitar line. The instruments provided the backbone for powerful but peaceful "oms" and other mantras. The music built throughout, never climaxing but flowing forward at rhythmic intervals, as reliably as a slow-moving, unceasing river.

That was the soundtrack vibrating through James McEwan's yoga class in a third-floor studio nestled among office buildings in the suburban parking lot of a grocery and liquor store. The rumblings of motorcycles and trucks encroached intermittently upon the simple serenity of the music. But no one inside seemed to mind.

When I first arrived, James was settling into his spot at the front of the class, and some of his students were quietly filtering in. He looked at home in this setting, having changed into a comfortable all-white cotton outfit. Still wearing his turban, he was intently organizing his materials for the class ahead.

James's kundalini yoga name is Sadhu Prem. It was given to him during yoga teacher training. "Prem means divine love, love of God, and Sadhu means master of spiritual practice," he explained. "It holds a vibration and represents when I'm in my sadhana [spiritual practice], when I'm living that, I'm feeling divine love of the Creator, so when I was given that name it just felt like an important part of something."

The kundalini James was on another plane. This was not the man I'd watched on YouTube for hours, throwing and withstanding the brutal force of bare-knuckle punches. That James was fighting for air, desperately thrashing to keep his head above water. This James was floating calmly on his back. It seemed natural. It made sense. It felt right.

The class filled up with about twenty students, more than I had been expecting for a Friday night. James circulated photocopied sheets of mantras the class would be using over the next hour.

"Sat Nam, everybody," McEwan began. "My name is Sadhu Prem, and it's an honour and a privilege to share these teachings with you tonight. Kundalini yoga is a really special tool. Really special teachings. We use breath—pranayam—sound and mantra, and movement asanas, all mixed in to have a powerful effect on our minds, bodies, spirits, or consciousness."

James led the class through the opening mantra, which translated to "I bow to the divine wisdom within." The exercises ranged from long, slow breathing to a practice called fire breath, which is a protracted series of short breaths delivered only through the nostrils. Throughout the class, James led chants of Sat Nam. This was not only his go-to chant but also his most heavily used inspirational piece, repeated within his teachings and instructions. "Sat means truth; Nam means name," McEwan explained to the class. "Truth is who I am, truth is my name."

James's voice and speaking rhythm were soothing and gentle but authoritative because of his knowledge and belief in the practice. With my eye keenly focused on the paradox that is James's past as a hockey enforcer and his present as a yoga instructor, I spotted more than a few obvious links to the precision focus, discipline, and determination that are required to compete on the ice.

About forty-five minutes into the class, during one of the most challenging intervals for his students (the prolonged fire breath portion), James delivered an inspirational speech. If not for the calm tone, flourishing metaphors, and accompanying sitar music, his words could easily have doubled as a pep talk from a head coach or team captain before a big game.

"Work with determination and work with compassion," he implored his students. "Listen to your body. You're the master of your body. If your body is saying stop, listen to that, respect your body. But then also, see where you can push yourself to grow. Have that balance. If you need to keep your arms straight, keep them straighter. You can do it. You have the strength within you. You have the whole power of creation within you. Like the rose coming up through the concrete. The power of the atom. The kundalini that is within you. You have that within you. Let's find a balance of that strength and that compassion."

As the class's most intense moments passed, James brought out his guitar and introduced one of his favourite mantras. His mood lightened, transforming from stern and discerning yoga teacher-cum-hockey-coach to a more boyish and slightly bashful campfire singalong leader.

"It's a very powerful mantra," he said. "It grants prosperity, happiness, and it says it even brings good luck to a scoundrel. So whatever karma, it's all good. Just chant this mantra. I started chanting this one and I can't stop smiling when I chant this. It feels really good to say."

James sang:

> Sa Re Sa Sa
> Sa Re Sa Sa Sa Rung
> Har Re Har Har
> Har Re Har Har
> Har Re Har Har Har Rung
> (That Infinite Totality is here, everywhere. That creativity
> of God is here, everywhere.)

The lilting guitar and the repeated chanting from the students seemed to have the intended effect, creating a warm and welcoming kumbaya feel. As the mantra continued on for more than ten minutes, even as an observer, I started to feel myself mentally floating away with the melody. And I was singing along too.

After the class, I caught up with some of James's students. They were calm, relaxed, and all smiles. Iwona Sienko, a woman in her forties, told me that, initially, she was surprised to learn that James had been a hockey fighter. "I almost couldn't imagine him being a hockey player," Iwona said. "But then there are so many kundalini yogis who are coming to this type of practice because we had some other different life stories that brings us to that centre of who we are."

Tessa Wetherill, a student that evening but also a yoga teacher colleague who first met James in kundalini training, acknowledged the effort and focus her friend put into his practice. "It's a hard thing to do to sit up there in front of other people and lead them into these things that are maybe very unfamiliar," she said. "You need to have integrity and really believe what you're saying, or else it comes off really badly. I admire what he's doing."

And Tessa, like her yoga classmates, took no issue with the fact that James used to bare-knuckle box on ice for a living. "We all have a past, and you bring that with you," she said. "It's not like anything ever gets erased. All of people's before lives, struggled lives ... it's all one thing. I could tell you things about me that would surprise you too. Just because we have these white things on our head [turbans], it makes us look so special, but we're just ordinary people trying to do it better every day."

What Iwona and Tessa were really saying was that James is a leader. You don't get to be the captain of a major junior hockey team by accident. He has always been focused, caring, forward-thinking, and task-oriented. James is a team builder. A believer in the power of the group's ability to achieve what the individual cannot. And although in the past he might have inspired his peers with a burst of explosive on-ice violence, he now inspires with a calm tone, self-assured aura, and sincere belief in a peaceful practice.

While those leadership skills that were honed on the ice were still a big part of James's post-fighting personality, for the most part, he had left hockey behind. He didn't watch much. Maybe a highlight pack here or there. And he hadn't been to the rink for a live game in more than a year. "I think it's a great game ... it obviously has a special place in my heart and will forever," McEwan said. "I watch it from a distance. But there's a love that will always be there, a love and respect for the game, because it brought me so many good things, so many good qualities that will serve me for the rest of my life and relationships."

But that break, that distance he'd been keeping from hockey, ended that night. James was set to revisit his old life with a return to the very arena where thousands of adoring fans once screamed and chanted his name as he fought for his team at centre ice.

There's probably no harder atmospheric turn you can experience than going from an ultra-calm evening at the yoga studio straight to the rink for a Friday night junior hockey game. Left behind are the soothing tones of the sitar, the mantras, and the breathing. Replacing them are the pounding beats of jock jam favourites, the gawky announcing of advertisements, the crashing of players against boards, the roaring of the fans, and the permeating scent of fried food and spilled beer. This is Prospera Place in Kelowna. This is Rockets hockey.

If McEwan was feeling any trepidation about revisiting his old stomping grounds, he wasn't showing it. Because he didn't have much time to change after his yoga class, James was still wearing his all-white attire and head covering. His black jacket slightly softened the starkness of the spiritual-attire-at-a-hockey-game conspicuousness. This was the same James I had observed at yoga, but now the backdrop was very different. It was wild to think that this man, known to his students only minutes before as Sadhu Prem, was once one of the most prolific fighters in Kelowna Rockets' history. And it all happened at this rink, in this town, in front of these fans.

But one of the first interactions James had upon returning to the rink was telling. It drove home the fact that, perhaps, he simply didn't belong here anymore. On his way through the parking lot, McEwan ran into someone he knew. (I wrongly assumed no one would recognize him because of the way he looked.) It was a former employee of the Kelowna Rockets, and although it may have been somewhat ancient history (nine years had passed), these two went way back. They spent the better part of two WHL hockey seasons working together, even travelling around Western Canada, Washington, and Oregon on long road trips. There would've been a time when these two knew each other very well, at least in a professional sense.

It took a long moment, but eventually, the old friend remembered James and they exchanged pleasantries. But then came the confusion.

"What's that thing on your head?" he asked.

James, no stranger to this line of questioning, responded simply, "It's a head covering."

Not quite satisfied, the former colleague persisted, "Is it a bandage?"

James said simply, "No."

It's one thing to be a fish out of water. It happens to pretty much all of us from time to time. But it's something completely different when the water is where you came from. When the water used to be home. When you feel alienated in the place where you used to be most comfortable, among teammates, friends, and family.

Despite the awkwardness, McEwan understands that although his journey has been challenging for him, it can be difficult for others to understand too.

"I get it, I can be practical," he said looking back at the interaction with his former colleague. "If you see someone and all of a sudden they're wearing a turban and you're in the West, that's not very common. If you see a Sikh or a Hindu, that's one thing. But to see a Western white man wearing a turban, it can turn some heads, especially if it's someone that you know. I can understand where that could be surprising for some people."

James and I took a seat behind the Rockets' net, in an empty swath about fifteen rows back from the ice. Despite all of the pain he's experienced, much of it rooted in this place, McEwan seemed to enjoy the familiarity and the buzz. "[I feel] the excitement ... You know, there's so much that happens in a game," he said. "I used to just sit right down there with season tickets with my brothers and my dad, so there's a lot of good memories and a lot of good energy at these games."

But James wasn't allowed to linger in the good reminiscence for long. The game was a choppy affair between the Kelowna Rockets and the visiting Portland Winterhawks. Lots of whistles for icing, offsides, and pucks out of play. Sloppy stuff. It was one of those games that reminds you that, despite the big crowd, the money being made, and the buzz in the air, the players are only teenagers. The vibe in the stands mirrored the disjointedness of the game. The crowd wasn't exactly laser focused, and who could blame them? Everything felt a bit off-kilter (maybe I was still recovering from the yoga-to-hockey shock).

At 6:06 of the second period, the dreariness of the game was split wide open by a burst of violence. There was a scrap. It was a familiar scene for James. A mid-ice bodycheck to the head. Gloves dropped. Crowd roared. Fists flew. As far as fights go, this one was pretty innocuous. Mostly a grappling battle. A jersey tug-of-war with the only landed punches glancing off the helmets and visors. Probably some sore hands to ice down post-game.

James applied the same philosophical approach to this fight as he did to his own when we were discussing them earlier at the tea shop. But this time, he took it a step further, to a place I wasn't expecting. "There's an understanding [of the fight], but there's also a concern," he said of his reaction. "There are solutions out there that we can find to channel that energy differently ... just start to find different ways to use that same energy because, from the core of it, it comes from a place of love."

Love? I was floored and immediately skeptical of the word in the context of two young men whose sole intention was to inflict as much physical pain upon one another as possible. From my perspective, as the anger explodes and the fists pound and the blood flows, love is nowhere in sight. Love isn't in the building. Love's probably not even in the same area code.

Hiding my incredulity as best as possible, I asked James to explain. He surprised me yet again, with an explanation that was both analytical and humane. "Love is a powerful emotion. It's at the heart of every warrior, and that's what these guys are, warriors out there," James told me. "And sticking up for one another, for a common goal, for that team, that family, that tribal instinct. When you look at even the enforcers and the protectors of the tribe, they'll put their lives on the line for the tribe. And so it's an honourable thing, and I have a lot of understanding, compassion, and respect for that. But also concern. I definitely felt it while I was doing it. Emotion of doing whatever I had to do for my teammates and the greater good, for the greater good of the family and the tribe."

After delving into the very core of McEwan's still-existent rationalization for the violence he perpetrated as a hockey fighter, we continued watching the game. The buzz from the fight continued into the second intermission, and we headed into what was set to be a much more energetic third period.

Once the Zamboni had flooded the ice surface and the new water froze, the third period began. And as so often happens in hockey, the initial fight begat another. At 5:54 of the third period, eighteen-year-old Kelowna winger Erik Gardiner and seventeen-year-old Portland centre Brad Ginnell squared off to exchange blows. In the eyes of British Columbia law, they were both children. Neither could drink legally and only one could vote.

Regan Bartel, the play-by-play broadcaster for AM 1150 in Kelowna, had the call: "And now we've got a fight at centre ... Brad Ginnell and Erik Gardiner of all people! Erik Gardiner trying to throw a right, DID! Ginnell takes a couple ... Now Ginnell right over the top, but Erik Gardiner will take down Ginnell ... Erik Gardiner with the victory!"

This fight was different from the first one. It was short but more freewheeling. Punches connected, mostly by Gardiner on Ginnell. It had some of that trademark McEwan recklessness to it. James was silent as the violence played out.

But the big moment came when, as the fight was ending, Gardiner fell forward onto Ginnell, smashing the back of his head into the ice (this did not appear to be intentional). The blood flowing from Ginnell's face spattered the electric-white ice with a deep crimson. Almost immediately, I saw a change in McEwan's body language. He sat up on the edge of his plastic blue seat. He's been there.

"I know, first of all, how it feels," McEwan said, eyes still focused sharply on Ginnell, who was slow to get up after what was certainly a sub-concussive trauma, if not a full-blown concussion. "Three things go on ... I'd say compassion, respect, but an alarming concern is overriding those other ones now." He knows how dangerous and catastrophic that final fall to the ice can be.

We continued to discuss the fight as James monitored the injured player and the replays on the scoreboard. "Look at that," he said, pointing intently. "His head bounces off the ice. That's how I got one of my last concussions ... my head whacking off the ice. And as you get older, it gets harder to bounce back, and it has devastating effects over and over. Messing with the brain is no joke, man, it's no joke. The brain can heal, but it takes a lot of work to undo that stuff."

It had been a long day retracing James's steps from idyllic small-town hockey kid with NHL dreams to junior and pro hockey fighter. On that journey, he accumulated all those injuries and all that damage, and finally came face-to-face with death, living to tell the tale only after finding spiritual meaning in an ancient plant-based brew and spiritual practice.

But despite everything he's been through, including multiple brushes with total destruction, when I asked James what, if anything, he would do over again if given the chance, his answer was blunt and, now that I know him, characteristic. His response seemed to reflect almost perfectly the two halves of himself: the hockey fighter with no regrets and the leave-it-all-on-the-ice absolutism, and the yogi with the belief that adversity is to be accepted, internalized, and expunged. It's to be breathed in and breathed out. Accepted and released.

"I wouldn't change anything because it's brought me to right here and right now and I feel very blessed and very grateful for everything," McEwan reflected defiantly. "Because it's in the challenges where I learned my biggest lessons and where the biggest change happened. I'm grateful for all the experiences, and especially the challenging ones. It's made life what it is right now, and I'm really grateful for life."

His reply was poetic but also practical. This kind of pervading mindset is required of him to continue, to stay alive, and (although it may only be proverbial this time around) to fight the good fight.

The game, notable mostly for its two fights and otherwise sloppy play, drew to a close. Portland Winterhawks 3, Kelowna Rockets 1. James and I exited the arena surrounded by throngs of fans, many ready to head home to bed, many others raring to keep the good times going at the local bars and clubs.

As we shook hands and said goodbye, I expected this intense daylong first meeting to be the last I would hear from James for at least a little while. Until the CBC Radio documentary went to air anyway.

As I unlocked my vehicle, bleary-eyed from a busy eighteen-hour day, I spotted a family of five crossing the street on the way back to their van. Mom, dad, and three kids, youngest around four and oldest maybe ten. I thought nothing of it. There were probably hundreds of kids at the game that night. Just another family outing to the good old hockey game.

But as it turned out, it wasn't nothing. James saw that family too. And for some reason the image stuck with him.

Only four days after our first meeting, James unexpectedly contacted me again. He was fired up and wanted to talk. The experience of revisiting his past, seeing the violence and the kids who witnessed it, had him looking at hockey fighting in a whole new light.

Gone was the talk of warriors and love and the implicit understanding of why the fighting happens. That whole mindset had been replaced with a much more strident tone. It was as though the pain of his own experience as a fighter was awakened by the sight of that family, by the kids who saw the fists flying and the blood spilling on the ice. James *was* those kids, watching other kids fight from the front row, internalizing the violence of Don Cherry's *Rock 'Em Sock 'Em* videos, being told, implicitly and explicitly, that this kind of violence is okay. That fighting is fine. And that the fighters themselves will also be fine.

James knows that none of that is true. And he knows it better than just about anyone else.

The whole experience had inspired McEwan's activist within, and in the days since the game, he'd written an open letter detailing his thoughts about hockey fighting and the culture that supports it. But as I began to read it, I realized that this piece of writing was much more than just a letter. This was James McEwan's manifesto. This was his transformative moment. He was no longer a former hockey fighter looking to share his tale in the hope that someone, somewhere might notice and make a change. He was now a fierce advocate against hockey fighting. Gone were the equivocations and the niceties. This was his line in the sand, his call to arms. James wrote emphatically, passionately, and absolutely. Paraphrasing or using select quotations would not do it justice. Here is James's letter letter, as sent to me, and read in part on CBC Radio, edited only slightly for clarity:

> It hit me like a ton of bricks as I walked down the street after we departed from Prospera Place post Rockets game. I was observing the people and fans leaving the game. There were families walking down the street together and there were little children laughing, playing and having fun. I looked at

these young children and saw their innocence and saw also how vulnerable they are. The parents and adults have such a responsibility in molding these children to who they will become as adults. The way they think and view the world comes in a huge way from their parents and environment they are brought up in. Especially young children.

Now, at that game there were two fights. And what happened after these fights? 6,000 people got up and cheered. I thought to myself, "What kind of message is this sending to these 5 year olds who see the parents and the whole culture praising and celebrating this?" Fighting is violence. Even if in a noble form. Right now the culture and environment in hockey is promoting violence. These kids will go home and remember that. It will become ingrained deep into their subconscious mind that not only is it ok to use violence, but it is rewarded. This is a sickness. A sickness of culture, and a sickness of the mind. An innocent child does not like fighting. If a fight broke out on the street and two adults started duking it out in front of these children, it would be a traumatic experience for them.

It's time for change. Letting violence continue in hockey and in our culture is very damaging. The long-term effects are devastating, with a disease like CTE and the mental and emotional trauma that is causing so much suffering and even causing players to kills themselves. It's time as a culture for us to grow and move in a positive direction. To continue letting violence happen in hockey through promoting it, praising it and having minimal penalties for it is like giving kids matches at a gas station and saying, "Have fun kids." In this hockey culture we have young boys praised and cheered for punching each other in the face while thousands pay money to watch.

It is time for the rule-makers, owners, promoters and people in positions of power to take the matches away from the kids and set some rules to make the game better and to protect the players. How many more lives need to be lost in tragedy for us to make things change?

In the interview I was asked what would I say to these young junior players coming up now, and I said I would share with them my story and let them decide.

I woke up the next morning and couldn't get that thought out of my mind. Here is why.

When I was playing, I was focused on a goal and would do whatever it took to achieve it. Receiving a black eye from a fight or even a foggy head was no way of stopping me. I was a young kid and unaware, I did not understand, I did not know the long-term effects of these actions. I did not know about CTE or about it causing brain damage and the suicides and the negative impact it has on life.

We knew concussions were harmful but not as much as we know now. We know now that the repeated hits to the head, big or small, are devastating and cause brain disease and tremendous mental and emotional damage. The culture promotes this and supports this right now. To me it is sick that it is ok for two young 16-year-old boys to have a space not only where it is socially accepted but cheered and praised to go punch each other in the face. It is even promoted and profits are being made from this. Even as a noble cause of standing up for a teammate, it is still sick. It's not healthy and the whole issue needs major healing.

So what would I say now to the players coming up? Yes, I would share my story and I would leave them with this message and not only to the players but the fans, the coaches, the owners, the media, the entire culture.

McEwan continued his appeal by addressing the people he sees as having the most power and influence to fundamentally change the sport of hockey. The players, the coaches, the business people, and the fans.

A message to the players

Fighting in hockey has devastating effects, I was close to killing myself multiple times and I truly believe there is a direct relation to the fights I have been in while playing hockey. Many hockey players have died from suicide, many are suffering right now and are very sick mentally, emotionally and physically due to hockey fighting. The latest science has shown the devastation hockey fights and consistent blows to the head, big and small blows, have on us. CTE is real and the players who have killed themselves had it. It's a disease that is directly related and caused by fighting and head shots.

Please stop this for your own good and for the example that you set for children and society. Please treat yourself, teammates and members of the other teams with respect and hold each other to a high standard of moral value and sportsmanship. You are warriors and have tremendous hearts, and the impact you have on our world is tremendous, more than you can even fathom right now. Be a true warrior of courage and integrity and make a stand for honour, peace and respect, on and off the ice.

A message to the rule-makers, owners, coaches, media and people in positions of power in hockey

I understand you work hard to make this game incredible and exciting for the players, fans and entire culture. I understand that you need to manage and run a sustainable business to keeps [*sic*] the game running and thriving. I also understand that many of you have children and you were once a small child, innocent and vulnerable.

Knowing now the devastation that these blows to the head caused not only by big concussions but also repeated blows to the head in fighting, I ask that you please help put a stop to this. Please help eliminate violence in hockey by making a stand and stop promoting it, rewarding it, praising it and letting it happen with minimal penalties. Please protect our players and our children coming up.

Some things that can be implemented right away to assist in eliminating violence in hockey: You can add major suspensions and fines to each fight, head shot and cheap shot. Make those penalties and fines even more hefty so that they hold players accountable to a high moral and ethical standard if they wish to play the game. I also recommend that you make the ice surface bigger. This will lessen the devastating hits. Players are skating on the same surface players have skated on for 100 years or so now. Guys are much bigger, stronger and faster, and we have way more advanced technology. When in a small closed area with this speed, damage is going to happen. Make the rink at least Olympic size or bigger. Do this and the game will be safer for the players, and even more entertaining for the fans. Change can be challenging, but it is necessary. Please have the courage to step up and make these changes right now. The lives of many are at stake.

A message to the fans and parents
You play a very important role in the game and the hockey culture. When you cheer and praise these fights, please remember you are also cheering and supporting the same thing that played a big role in taking the lives of players like Rick Rypien, Derek Boogaard, Steve Montador and many more. You cheering for fighting is supporting an act that causes major physical, mental and emotional illness and suicide to the players. Your [*sic*] are also supporting and promoting violence to every child that is in attendance watching at the rink, online or on TV. Most of you have families and would never want your own child to get CTE and have a terrible disease that causes them to take their own life and potentially the lives of others. I ask you to have the honour and courage to stop cheering for fights. I ask you to sit down and turn your back to these fights. Please help set a good example for our children that violence is not okay. These children are our future and we have a responsibility to them. It's time to learn from our mistakes and raise them in a way that will help us create a better world for all. Let's educate them and teach them about honour and peace by setting this example.

James McEwan's powerful plea, based on his first-hand experience of on-ice violence and the devastating fallout, did not end with the airing of a CBC Radio documentary and the publishing of an online article. With those stories reaching hundreds of thousands of people across the country and around the world, he gained notoriety. Sure, there were the detractors (probably some of the same folks you may remember from the Twitter comments earlier). But there was also an outpouring of love and support. Here are just a few of the comments that followed after he shared the CBC article on his Facebook page:

Jeff Artiss: "Here for you brother. Had no idea, and appreciate the honesty and journey you shared. Let the light shine and be that example."

Christine Marie: "Amazing the work you are doing and the being you keep on becoming, proud of you for being brave and sharing. be well my friend x."

Trish Ellis: "Great story James. It's awesome you're bringing light to a topic that warrants it. So glad you weathered the storm. You are clearly using your experience for your greater evolution. I know you are making a huge difference on this earth. Much love to you my friend."

Derek Couture (former major junior and minor pro hockey player from 2000–15): "Nice, I'm glad you shed that 'tuff hockey player' mentality, where we show no pain and battle our demons in private. You been able to share your story and asked for help, which I believe to be the real strength. Take care my fellow warrior."

It wasn't only James's friends, fans, and colleagues who were surprised to learn about the severity of his struggles. Although his family were aware that he faced some difficulties near the end of his playing career, none of them seemed to really understand just how serious those health issues were, and how close he had come to death. James's brother Joshua, who is now a coach at a hockey camp in Kelowna, said he was floored by the revelations in the CBC story.

"I listened to that interview," said the youngest of the three McEwan brothers, "and then I was like, 'I didn't know he was thinking of taking his own life.' It wasn't until then that I actually realized it." Joshua told me that he felt an incredible sadness when he learned his brother was struggling with thoughts of suicide. And Joshua believes that James probably has CTE, but just like everyone else, he can't be sure.

James's mother, Brenda McEwan, said she had a sense that things weren't going well for her son near the end of his playing days in the ECHL but didn't know just how dire the situation had become. "I moved out to Prince George and he came out there for a visit and I noticed that then a little," she told me from her hometown of Kamloops, BC. "I honestly didn't know the severity of how bad it was. It still really upsets me. James was the type who thought, 'I'm grown, I can handle this,' but he was really all alone out there, and that is so heart-wrenching for me. He's your son."

As the dangerous scope of James's brain injuries and mental health issues became clearer, Brenda wondered why she didn't find out earlier. "I asked him. I said, 'James, why didn't you call us, either me or dad or somebody? Why didn't you reach out to us?'" she recounted, becoming emotional. "He said, 'Mom, I didn't know what was wrong with me.' As a mother, it's very hard to sit back and watch when you see that child that was super happy and always full of life, and that kid comes home and you're like, 'Okay, what's going on?' and you can't fix it. That's tough. As a parent we're supposed to fix things for our kids, and when we can't, then you go to your faith."

Brenda says finding out about the massive changes in James's lifestyle that involved ayahuasca and kundalini yoga was difficult to understand, at least at first. "I was thrown back by it because people are like, 'Why is your son wearing a turban?'" she said. "If that's what's going to heal you, I don't care what you wear. This is what's going to make you better. And then he started to study, and I actually supported him one hundred percent, and I started to attend some of these yoga events he's putting on, and you know what, they are amazing."

Like his mother, Joshua McEwan supports his brother's new approach to life. Despite James's health challenges, the youngest McEwan is confident that, with his brother's new-found outlook, he'll be able to cope well and continue to not only survive but thrive. "I have faith that he's going to be okay and that he's supported," Joshua said. "I don't really worry about it because I think it's part of what he's dealing with right now, and I think he's taking decent precautions. Especially as of late, taking care of himself to be able to deal with this properly."

Now, you might be wondering what the WHL and the Kelowna Rockets think about McEwan's story and his decision to share it so publicly, laced with such terse criticism of hockey fighting. After all, James was not some feral fighting hooligan the likes of which was cartoonishly immortalized in movies like *Slap Shot* and *Goon*. He was a devoted teammate and a pillar of his community. He was a leader who believed in the sport of hockey and his particular role within it. McEwan strove to lift people up, on and off the ice. He was the captain of the Kelowna Rockets. He was a fan favourite.

With that in mind, I got Bruce Hamilton, the owner of the Rockets, on the phone. He spoke curtly and gruffly. It was very old-school hockey. I could almost imagine a legendary executive like Harold Ballard or Glen Sather on the other end of the line, smoking a cigar.

The moment the conversation began, Hamilton was confrontational and direct: "What is it that you're trying to do here?" he asked, his tone suggesting I was up to no good.

I explained that I wanted to ask questions about one of his former players and about fighting in junior hockey.

"All right, but I'm not going to have much to say about it," he warned.

Once the conversation got going, Hamilton lightened up and became much more open, if not candid. He remembered James McEwan well: the heart, the leadership, the fighting and all.

"That was James's game. The skill side of it wasn't his game," Hamilton said. "His game was to try to be an intimidating player out there, and that part of the game is gone today. He was an ultra-competitive guy. He was the ultimate teammate. He's a guy that is very interesting. I like him a lot. I'm glad that he's finding the right path here for himself. It does [concern me]. I don't know if it's all related to hockey."

When it came to getting a comment from the WHL, its representative was unwilling to address McEwan's story specifically, but I was able to ask some general questions about fighting in the league.

WHL vice-president of hockey Richard Doerksen told me fighting is down (it is, currently), and the league is happy with that. "Fights do occur. What we're trying to really work on are the unnecessary fights, the staged fights," he said. "I guess hockey has had the feeling in the past that if two players want to settle their differences for whatever reason, whether it was a hit that was borderline or a hit on a teammate, that that has been a part of the game, and we continue to have discussions on that aspect."

When Doerksen said "unnecessary fights" what he meant was fights for the sake of fighting. Where two players drop the gloves for the show of it. To ignite the fans' excitement and get their teammates going. By that same logic, I would think a "necessary fight" would be one that involved retribution, the perceived protection of teammates.

Doerksen is certainly right on at least one front. Between 2007 and 2017, fighting in the WHL was cut nearly in half. So, clearly some progress has been made. But fights in the WHL are now occurring at nearly twice the rate as they do in the NHL. This seems counterintuitive, considering the WHL prides itself on and is paid lucrative development fees for being a top breeding ground for NHL talent. Why does fighting happen twice as often in a league for kids when the adults they're supposed to be mimicking are doing it half as often?

James's message was out there. His story had permeated the hockey ether. The power-brokers were aware of what he had gone through, but they were not compelled to act.

James's decision to speak out may have ruffled more than a few feathers in the hockey community, but it also caught the eye of folks like-minded in their criticism of the violence that pervades the sport. The fledgling World Association of Ice Hockey Players Unions (WAIPU) connected James with a labour union in Oregon State called the American Federation of Labor and Congress of Industrial Organizations (AFL-CIO). The union wanted help in its fight with the WHL's Portland Winterhawks.

The owners of the Winterhawks wanted similar labour exemptions in Oregon that had been given to other major junior teams in Washington State, BC, Saskatchewan, Manitoba, New Brunswick, Nova Scotia, and Prince Edward Island. Those exemptions give the teams the right to pay the players sub-minimum wages, and to stop them from accessing workers' compensation and unemployment rights. The argument is that the players should be considered amateur athletes, not professionals, and should, therefore, not qualify for those labour protections.

The bill (Bill HB4093) passed quite easily through Oregon's House of Representatives, but then the labour movement found out about it. The unions didn't like it, so they got ahold of James, and he was more than up for another chance to advocate for himself and junior players who have shared his experiences.

So, on a cold February morning in 2018, James packed his best suit and tie and jumped on a plane to Portland. He was set to testify in front of the Oregon State Senate. McEwan had already shared his story on multiple national platforms in Canada, and now he was en route to speak his truth in the annals of power in the United States.

When James appeared before the politicians who make up Oregon's Senate Committee on Workforce, he was calm and resolute. He spoke slowly and intensely. And just like every time McEwan ever stepped on the ice, he didn't hold back, delivering a forceful and highly critical testimony.

"In the WHL, children ... young players ... seventeen, sixteen years old, are being abused, manipulated, exploited, and neglected," he testified. "The consequences of allowing and tolerating fighting and violence in the game, in hockey, is utterly devastating, and having the power to stop the violence and let it continue because it profits a small group is cowardly and disgusting. The NHL and WHL continue to make excuses to let the violence and abuse and exploitation continue."[4]

This kind of all-out attack was new territory for James. "Cowardly." "Disgusting." "Abuse." "Exploitation." These weren't words that I was accustomed to hearing from him. In our interviews, James had always taken time and care to consider the other side. To credit the owners, administrators, and rule makers for their role in packaging and promoting the game. To implore them, with kindness and positivity, to change the game for the better. His previous messages were always peppered with an overarching theme of unity and a shared love for the game.

Not this time.

James's powerful and pointed testimony, along with the words of fellow former player Tyler Maxwell, had a strong impact on the committee, in particular, Oregon State Senator Sara Gelser, who spoke to the players as the proceedings were coming to a close.

"I want to apologize," she said. "I took my daughter to a Winterhawks game, and it did not occur to me that we were enjoying an evening and having fun based on the exploitation of other children that were her age, and I am very remorseful that we participated in that, and I'm very, very sorry for what you experienced."[5]

The bill was referred to the Senate Rules Committee, but then the legislature was adjourned for the season, so the bill died on the vine. McEwan, Maxwell, and the AFL-CIO had been successful, at least for the time being.

But the Oregon story didn't end there. The emotionally charged testimony caught the attention of the media with headlines like:

- "WHL and Junior Hockey Get Much More Than They Bargained for in Gambit with Oregon Lawmakers" in the *Hockey News*
- "Ex-Tip Critical of His Treatment by the Team and the WHL" in the *Everett (Washington) Daily Herald*
- "WHL to Examine Allegations by Former Players of Scholastic Fraud, Refusal of Medical Treatment" on TSN.ca

The WHL had been watching the Oregon proceedings closely and didn't like what it heard. The league wanted to investigate these serious allegations levelled by former players and put them to rest. In pretty much every media report, the WHL said it was surprised, disappointed, and concerned by the statements. So concerned, in fact, that the league's legal counsel hired retired Royal Canadian Mounted Police (RCMP) deputy commissioner Craig Callens to look into the claims. The league refers to Callens's investigation as an independent one, but that is untrue given that it was paid for by lawyers who are paid by the WHL.

Nevertheless, the retired deputy commissioner went about the investigation, he says, interviewing more than fifty people who were described by the league as coaches, billet family members, administrators, and others familiar with the players and their experiences. The players who testified in Oregon opted not to make themselves available to Callens, anticipating that he would be biased against them. The report was not made public because the WHL said it wanted to protect the confidentiality of those interviewed. Instead of publishing the report in full, the investigator posted a summary of his findings.

"There is no evidence to suggest that [the players' testimonies] are a reflection of the typical experience of a WHL player," Callens writes. "All three had aspirations of playing hockey at the highest possible level. Each of the players went on to play professional hockey after the WHL."

"The review revealed that [the WHL has] a significant number of comprehensive and modern policies and programs in place that support player development, health and wellness, and post-secondary education," Callens continued. "Our review concluded that the issues identified by Tyler Maxwell, James McEwan and Kim Taylor were not systemic to the League or to a particular team. In all but one of the cases, the players were either aware of the terms of the agreements or there was insufficient, and at times no, evidence to establish the allegation."[6]

The report was unabashedly one-sided. In Callens's opinion, the players' testimonies were absolutely, without question untrue.

When I interviewed WHL commissioner Ron Robison, he said that he felt the report absolved the league, and emphasized that he and others within the WHL were vindicated by the findings.

"The information was considered to be false, and consequently, we take offence to that," Robison said. "We pride ourselves, first and foremost, on providing our players with a safe and positive experience. And the WHL's reputation was damaged by their comments, so I think the method in which we went through this by having an independent investigation points out that virtually all these allegations were false at the time of the hearing."

Because Robison used the phrase "the WHL's reputation was damaged," I was quick to ask him if the league was considering legal action against its own former players.

After a lengthy pause, he said no but left his options open. "Not at this point," he said. "We'll just focus on really trying to educate them better on what the players' experience is all about."

For James McEwan, the report represented another setback. He had given his all to the testimony, just as he had to everything else in his hockey career, and in his life. He had travelled to another country and laid his soul bare in front of not only politicians but also, once again, the entirety of the hockey world. To be told that there was no evidence to back up his painful personal experiences was a bitter pill to swallow. James knew that the hockey world was an exclusive club that protected itself fiercely from outside critics—he used to be a part of that club. What he wasn't expecting was to be called everything short of a liar.

The Callens report rattled McEwan and pushed him to reconsider his decision to challenge hockey's status quo and the power-brokers who enforce it. But in the end, it just made him angrier.

"From my experience and from my eyes and how I'm seeing the world, fighting and violence causes harm to people, and allowing it to happen is neglecting to make the necessary changes that need to happen to protect the players," James told me after the report was released, sounding uncharacteristically flustered. "Everything that I said is a hundred percent true. We know that CTE exists.

[We know] what happens when you get punched in the head, and it doesn't even have to be a big concussion. They're allowing it to happen. If that's not neglect then ... you know ... look it up in the dictionary."

The Oregon experience showed James that, in the pursuit of change, speaking his personal truth about hockey is more than just speaking with a reporter, or posting on social media, or putting on a suit to speak to an interested group of politicians. Simply put, whistle-blowing is hard. And it's exhausting. It's a lot like something else James has become intimately familiar with throughout his life.

Taking on the hockey establishment and challenging Canada's sacred cow is a full-tilt, gloves-off donnybrook of a bare-knuckle brawl. And as with some of the biggest proverbial brawls out there, it looked as though this one would be fought in the courts. (Although that metaphor certainly fits the narrative, James maintains that he's pursuing the court action from a stance of peace and justice.)

There are many ways of trying to get a powerful group of people to listen to you and do what you want. You can gather signatures on a petition. You can rally at their head offices. You can write letters to your political representatives. You can speak in the media. You can find ways to influence their customers or shareholders. You can protest with marches and blockades. You can revolt. Some methods are a bit more passive than others, but all are admirable and legitimate ways of trying to effect change.

But this is James McEwan we're talking about here. He of the 200-plus career fights. He who would never back down from a scrap no matter the size of the opponent. He, the thrower of haymakers. James McEwan, the man who so often in a fight seemed to lack that gene for self-preservation. James knows one way to fight, and that's all out. So it will probably surprise no one to learn that in his struggle to change the game of hockey, and to protect his fellow warriors from the devastation of brain injuries that brought him repeatedly to the brink of death, James threw a bomb.

McEwan became the lead plaintiff in a class-action lawsuit against the Canadian Hockey League (CHL), the Western Hockey League, and Hockey Canada. Notice of that lawsuit was filed in the Supreme Court of British Columbia on January 9, 2019. McEwan is the lead representative for "any and all former and current players in the CHL who did not play in the NHL and suffered injury as a result of concussive and sub-concussive impacts to the head during a 'hockey activity.'" In other words, anyone who played major junior, or blue-collar professional hockey, and was hurt on the job, just like McEwan.

The lawsuit outlines all of the same hardships and challenges McEwan has faced post-hockey, including anxiety, stress, severe mood swings, depression, anger, fatigue, and suicidal thoughts. It lays out McEwan's current reality starkly, saying, "These symptoms are still active presently." It claims James's injuries were "caused or contributed to by the negligence and/or breach of statutory duty of the CHL, the WHL, and employees of the leagues." It claims the leagues didn't sufficiently warn teams and players about the long-term risks of repeated head trauma, that they did not launch appropriate concussion awareness campaigns, that they did not enforce acceptable concussion protocols, that they promoted and glorified increased violence between players, and that they allowed fighters like McEwan to continue playing when the leagues knew, or ought to have known, that they suffered a traumatic brain injury.[7]

The lawsuit was months in the making, and McEwan was happy with the timing. He was able to rest and recover from his last foray into advocacy, which caused him a great deal of frustration and pain.

"It feels like a good thing," McEwan stated simply. "It feels like the right thing to do. How it's all unfolded, from speaking with you, from speaking with the lawyers, I didn't go out looking for any of it. It just kind of came to me, and I've just told my truth the best that I can. My intention is to make the world a better place and hockey is a big part of our culture, and an important part. It was a big part of my life and that's my hope with this, is just to make positive change for the generations to come and to help anyone who's been hurt by these things."

Throughout his career, James McEwan proved repeatedly that he was willing to stand up for himself and others. And with this lawsuit, and in putting a group of very powerful and influential hockey people on notice, he's showing once again that he won't back down. Not from anyone.

McEwan's words critical of fighting and the hockey establishment, recorded in the CBC stories, delivered in front of the politicians in Oregon, and written into the lawsuit, have not come without consequences. Although he's received many messages of love and encouragement for the positive change he's pursuing, some who still participate in the hockey industry have distanced themselves from him.

James made part of his living training young hockey players, but because of his challenges, that work fell away for a while. In 2018, James returned to the work and helped train a young player who was heading into the junior ranks, just as he did himself all those years ago. He enjoyed the familiarity of the process and drew satisfaction from the relationship building. He wanted more. James has big ideas for folding his new-found spiritual practices into traditional hockey training. He wants to use meditation to help players focus and develop leadership and character. He wants to use yoga to help build more resilient bodies.

So McEwan called a former hockey colleague who was coaching minor hockey and had previously offered him the opportunity to help out. James wanted to get out on the ice for some volunteer work, so he called, texted, and emailed. No response. He reached out to a major midget team to volunteer. No coaches needed, he was told. He tried multiple teams in West Kelowna, a suburb of Kelowna. No dice. James couldn't get a callback. He felt like he'd been blacklisted, and he was frustrated.

"Man, I'm a former captain there," he said. "And I feel like I've been getting the cold shoulder from the hockey community. It hasn't been a good feeling."

The truth of the matter is that James is a whistle-blower. And what so often happens to whistle-blowers is happening to James. It plays like a classic Hollywood movie. Young, passionate upstart has the courage and strength of conviction to speak out against injustice, to fight for what he believes is right. But change never comes easy. On cue, the establishment, those who believe in it and those who aspire to be a part of it, not only rejects his ideas but also rejects him. Many of these folks want nothing to do with James. To so many in the hockey community, because he chose to take aim at the game they love, he's become an outcast. To this particular group of people, hockey is Canada's national game, and it doesn't really matter how passionate, articulate, and, above all, right James might be. He represents change, and for many that's simply too much to stomach. It's risky and scary.

But why does James care what the hockey establishment thinks of him? He's moved on to yoga and music and activism. To a better way of life. Why does he care about the politics of small-town hockey?

The truth is, no matter how hard he tries, McEwan just can't quit the game—it's in his blood. The cold, smooth ice, the feel of the puck on the blade, the coach's whistle, the locker-room banter. And it always seems to draw him back. It's almost as though hockey and James have a codependent relationship—he's the atom's nucleus and hockey the ever-circling electron, attached to him and his life by electromagnetic force.

McEwan is no longer a hockey player, but he still feels a connection, a longing to be around the game. That symbiotic relationship persists, as always.

But he's preaching ideas of peace, harmony, and mindfulness within a sporting culture that still values violence. He's pushing for a change that, although it may be coming sometime in the distant future, the game is unwilling to accept. For now anyway.

Despite the fact that James has found other passions and believes deeply in them, it still hurts him to know that his activism has resulted in some level of excommunication from the hockey world.

"It's probably guiding me into the areas that I want to be going anyway, my yoga, my music," he said. "I know after that article came out and the stuff in Portland ... now it's like, I can't even get a volunteer position helping kids?!"

When it comes to hockey, James McEwan now inhabits a place in between. He's stuck in hockey purgatory. James is in the neutral zone doing endless Russian ladder drills, blue line to blue line.

James loves the game, and appreciates the journey it's led him on, but it appears as though the game might not love him back. Considering all that he's been through, maybe it never did.

For now, it appears as though James McEwan will have to take his passion for the game of hockey and all that it left him with, including the devastating brain injuries, and forge a completely different path. He's excited to be opening a camp called Infinite Ice for young hockey players in his hometown of Terrace with his brother Joshua. The camp focuses on all of the hockey necessities: the skating, the shooting, the passing, the scoring. But it also goes multiple steps further. It encourages the elevation of consciousness. It promises to unite players with their inner power to be connected, balanced, and strong. It preaches leadership and sustainability and character development that will extend beyond the ice surface. And fighting will most certainly not be a part of it.

But despite that, James is still only dipping his toe back into the hockey waters. So far, the camp is planned to run for a single week. He will continue to spend most of his time away from the game. And in his time off the ice, James will continue to live and to heal. Away from the roaring crowds. Away from that unmistakable feel of steel cutting through ice. Away from the friendship and the brotherhood. Away from the game to which he gave everything.

But to James, it's worth it. Because while he's away, he'll continue his fight to change hockey, and to prevent future players from falling into the trap he did, from dropping the gloves, from suffering devastating injuries, and from flirting with CTE and the black abyss of death. To stop them from falling into a life of bare-knuckle boxing on ice.

CHAPTER 5
CTE: YOU'LL ONLY KNOW WHEN YOU'RE DEAD

Right off the hop, Frazer McLaren's gonna go with Dave Dziurzynski
... McLaren dropped Dziurzynski ... and he's out. McLaren's gonna end
up going to the Leaf locker room as well, he's cut on the chin. But the
concern, of course is with Dziurzysnki, who is gonna be helped off the
ice ... Always disturbing to see a player like that, whether you're a fan
of it or not.

—Frazer McLaren vs. Dave Dziurzynski
(Toronto Maple Leafs vs. Ottawa Senators, March 6, 2013)

IT'S JUST floating there.

It's surrounded by cerebrospinal fluid. Attached to the body only by the brain stem, which extends downward to become the spinal cord.

There it is, lighting up, with billions upon billions of neurons firing like a glorious cascade of shooting stars.

The human brain is the focal point of the central nervous system. It controls our organs, our muscles, our hormones.

It's a biological computer. And it's a goddamn wonder.

And it's just floating there.

But then ... BAM.

A fellow fighter delivers a devastating bare-fisted blow to the head.

The skull is jolted by the blow. The brain moves because it is, in fact, just floating there, mostly unfixed inside the skull.

The movement is where the harm happens. In some cases, the brain smashes against the inside of the skull. The smashing can happen more than once, on rebound from the first impact (on the front of the skull, then on the back), depending on the severity of the blow. Those inside-the-skull collisions damage the brain.

And if it's not the actual impact that causes the hurt, it's the torqueing and twisting that happen to the brain as a result of movement from the punch. That contortion shears and shreds the brain's delicate fibres. It hurts just thinking about it.

That right there is the simplest way of describing a concussion. And the thing is, concussions beget concussions. When players return to play before healing fully from one concussion, they're susceptible to another. They're perhaps a small step slower than usual, still fighting through the fog left behind by the previous trauma.

And when it comes to fighting in hockey, it's young players, at the junior level, who are at the greatest risk of not only suffering concussions in the first place but of becoming reinjured. That's because the brain is extra vulnerable in its early stage of development, and the young brain takes so much longer than the mature brain to recover from traumatic injury.

Dr Naznin Virji-Babul is an expert on brain injuries in young people. She's a neuroscientist and associate professor in the Department of Physical Therapy at the University of British Columbia in Vancouver.

"We used to think that the brain was fully developed by the time you were three, four, or five," Virji-Babul told me. "And now we know that brain development, especially the areas around your frontal cortex that are responsible for things like your memory, your impulse control, your risk-taking behaviour, all of these kinds of behaviours, are still under development. So we're dealing with a brain that is sort of under construction still. I often give the analogy that if you were building a house and the top layer wasn't built, and you had an earthquake, the whole foundation of the house is affected by that."

And we may not have even a tenuous grasp on possibly the most important, and potentially dangerous, aspect of youth brain injuries. Again, this comes down to the continuing brain development underway in young people. The brain is so plastic and malleable in this stage that injuries can often physically change the brain forever. It's like kneading a ball of Play-Doh and then trying to return the blob to exactly its previous shape.

"If children or adolescents get an injury during this very vulnerable phase, it's actually a little more risky than it is for an adult, whose brain is already developed," Dr Virji-Babul continued. "We can see in our research that once a child has an injury and has symptoms for a long time, we see that their brain actually seems to be reorganized even as a result of a single injury. The big question that we don't know ... is this plasticity, is this reorganization that we've seen in the brain ... is that just as good as what the kid had functionally before? Or are there subtle changes in their cognitive function that we should be worried about?"

But just because brain injuries can be more dangerous for young athletes doesn't mean they can't be devastating for players of all ages. When a player sustains multiple concussions, that can lead to the neurodegenerative disease James McEwan and other former hockey fighters believe they could be suffering from: chronic traumatic encephalopathy, or CTE. And that's where things get really serious.

Scientists have yet to pinpoint the exact underlying causes of CTE, but they know that repeated brain injuries lead to progressive degeneration of brain tissue. That degeneration is often marked by an abnormal form of a protein known as tau. Tau is a complex protein that is a normal constituent of the brain's nerve fibres, or axons.

Dr Charles Tator is probably the most celebrated neurosurgeon in Canada. He's a member of the Order of Canada and Canada's Sports Hall of Fame, and he's the project director of the Canadian Sports Concussion Project at the Krembil Neuroscience Centre at the Toronto Western Hospital in Ontario. He explains that brain trauma causes phosphate groups to accumulate within the tau protein. "These little buggers called phosphates come along, attach to the tau protein and disable this protein," Dr Tator told me. "It can no longer perform its function, and its function is to aid in the transmission of impulses from one nerve cell to another ... Eventually, the cell dies. So it's like a poisonous material in the cell."

Scientists also know that CTE is particularly tricky in that it can be terribly non-linear. Changes in the brain can begin months, years, or decades after the last traumatic brain injury. Dr Tator says it's the unpredictable nature of CTE that makes it so difficult to understand. "We don't know how it happens except that it happens when you have multiple blows [to the head]," he said. "We don't really know whether it takes concussions or sub-concussions, or both, to produce it ... and we know for example that some people can take hundreds of blows and not end up with CTE. So there is a huge individual variation to consider." Many scientists believe that there is very likely to be a genetic element to CTE, which only complicates the matter further.

We know that concussions can lead to CTE but so can sub-concussive impacts. A hockey player doesn't even need to be hit in the head to be at risk of developing the disease. A solid check that jostles the body. A hard collision with the boards. The glancing blow of a fist. Even if a player doesn't perceive that they've received a brain injury, that doesn't mean the damage and the subsequent degeneration isn't happening.

And while the precise way CTE takes form is still quite muddy, the results are much more clear. The brain is devastated. Neurons are lost; brain tissue is scarred. The brain loses weight because of atrophy.

Dr Tator has examined forty-five donated brains through his work with the Canadian Sports Concussion Project, including that of former NHLer Steve Montador, who died in 2015 and, because of Tator's autopsy, was later discovered to have CTE. Dr Tator says the brain with CTE is not pretty to look at. "It makes a mess of the brain, and it ends up looking like a graveyard," he said. "Because there's no normal surviving neurons when it's in its worst form."

That all sounds bad. But it's the symptoms that are even more devastating. CTE can lead to mental health issues including depression and anxiety. It can spur violent behaviour because of impaired judgment and lack of impulse control. That violence is usually directed at the people who care about the CTE sufferer most. CTE is associated with a risk of developing Parkinson's disease and with dementia. The desperate need to dull the roaring discomfort of CTE can also lead to self-medication: substance use and eventually addiction. Perhaps worst of all, many athletes who are known to have lived with CTE have died by suicide, just as reports suggest Rick Rypien and Wade Belak did. If CTE doesn't kill you, it just might make you kill yourself instead.

As if all of the above wasn't enough, possibly the most complicated and devastating part about CTE is that you can't find out for sure if you actually have it. At this time, a CTE diagnosis can only be determined with a post-mortem biopsy. When it comes to a disease that delivers cruel irony upon cruel irony, perhaps the cruellest of all is that you have to be dead to know if it was CTE that was killing you.

And if *that* irony isn't cruel enough, think about this: without the ability to diagnose CTE in living humans, there is no way to develop a treatment for the disease. How can doctors even begin to determine what kinds of treatments or therapies might be effective in treating a disease in a real, live patient, if they have no way of knowing whether that patient has the disease in the first place? That mind-bending proposition illustrates the current medical quagmire facing the players who have an inkling that they might be living with CTE. There are no options. There is only sickness, worry, and uncertainty.

Despite this dire situation, there's hope and momentum building in the scientific community in regards to CTE research. Recently, there's been progress when it comes to diagnosing CTE in living people.

Dr Bennet Omalu, the doctor who is now most famous for being played by Will Smith in the film *Concussion*, and for being the loudest and most insistent whistle-blower about brain injuries in the National Football League (NFL), has continued his work in the field. Now in the Department of Pathology and Laboratory Medicine at the University of California, Davis, Omalu published an article in the medical journal *Neurosurgery* in November 2017 about diagnosing CTE in living patients.[8]

Dr Omalu and his team used a molecular imaging probe that crosses the blood-brain barrier and binds to abnormal proteins in the brain. The images were taken about four years before the patient died (CNN reports that the patient was former NFL player Fred McNeill, whose family believed he was living with CTE). The binding levels of the imaging probe were compared to the levels of tau found in the patient's brain after Omalu conducted the post-mortem examination. In the end, the scientists compared the known levels of tau to the distribution of the binding agent. The numbers lined up. This study established that this particular method of probing the brain ([F-18]FDDNP-PET, to be exact) could be fruitful in identifying tau buildup in living patients, eventually allowing for diagnoses of CTE in living people. Further study is required.

Another promising finding comes from a team at Boston University that includes Dr Ann McKee, a BU School of Medicine professor of neurology and pathology, director of the school's CTE Center, and another legend in the field. She worked alongside Dr Jonathan Cherry, a post-doctoral fellow. Dr McKee, Dr Cherry, and their fellow researchers found a possible biomarker, or red flag, that could be used to diagnose CTE in the living. Research on a protein known as CCL11 has shown that it might be not only an effective biomarker but also a way for doctors to differentiate between CTE and Alzheimer's before death. (The two degenerative diseases share a number of symptoms and physical similarities in the brain.)

"Looking in the brain tissue of people who were diagnosed with CTE, and comparing that to people who've never played sports before, or people with Alzheimer's disease, we saw that the protein CCL11 was elevated only in those people with CTE," Dr Cherry told me of their post-mortem findings. "We then followed up and looked at the spinal fluid, which is a much more attractive area to look at biomarkers, and we saw the same thing. So potentially, that CCL11 might be able to distinguish people that have CTE from just normal aging or people with other diseases."

Although CCL11 can be detected in living patients, Dr Cherry and his team don't expect that protein to be the be-all, end-all biomarker for identifying CTE. But it could be one in a set of five to eight markers (still to be identified) that leads to diagnosis. He says the work must be repeated many times, especially with living samples. "We can't learn a lot about the disease with just post-mortem tissue," Dr Cherry said. "So the way therapies work is we have to identify [CTE] in living people so that when we actually start treating people, and see if they get better or worse because we can't tell who has it while they're alive. So all these clinical trials that are going to be started, we're never going to know if the trials work or not until they die, and we really have no reference point from there. So we have to identify it in life so we can better understand how to treat it."

Dr Cherry is confident in the possibility of receiving answers to these questions soon. He believes definitive work on CTE diagnosis and treatment is coming in the next five to ten years.

One of my biggest concerns about the fact that CTE cannot currently be diagnosed in the living is more philosophical than medical. In talking to aspiring young hockey players for this book, I found that the uncertainty and imprecision surrounding the medical science on CTE has led not to trepidation and cautiousness, as one might expect, but more to dismissal. For many players, the fact that CTE cannot be pinpointed provides an excuse to ignore the possible devastation that may await them. They push it down the road. If you only find out after you die, why worry now?

I asked Dr Cherry if solid diagnostic science might lead to CTE being taken more seriously by athletes.

"Yeah, it definitely would because you'd put a face on it. It makes it real," he answered. "It's not just something you can say, 'Well, who knows?' It'll be a real diagnosis. There's a lot of fear behind that, but once we get this real diagnosis, we can actually start to create therapies for it."

The good news is that scientists are working feverishly to decipher the dark world of CTE, especially in the sporting world. But to say those scientists are playing a desperate game of catch-up would be an understatement. This is like being down 6–1 heading into the third period. It's a big hole. If you focus, you can see that winning is achievable. But that vision of victory is hazy and the path to success daunting.

We know that many former hockey players, like James McEwan, are exhibiting symptoms of the disease. But just as troubling is the fact that every time a current player incurs a traumatic brain injury, whether in professional or minor hockey, the seed of CTE is sown. And that seed may one day germinate into depression, anxiety, anger, violence, and maybe even suicide. Simply put, CTE is suffering, for the players who live with it and for the people who love them.

And although the men featured in this book might never know if they have chronic traumatic encephalopathy, the same will not be true for future generations of hockey players. There's a good chance that, by the time they're ready to compete in the upper echelons of hockey, the five-year-olds now lacing up and taking to the ice for the first time will have a clear vision of what CTE is, and they'll be able to find out if they have it. And, even more hopefully, there may be a treatment, or treatments, available not long after that. As Dr Cherry said, more definitive knowledge and understanding of CTE will change not only the way hockey players play the game but also the way they view the game. Hell, it might even stop them from playing before they ever start.

The future of contact sport is inextricably linked to the future of CTE research. The more information that is discovered, the more those sports will have to evolve to reflect that discovery, however slowly, however reluctantly. Whatever form those findings take, whether five or fifteen years down the road, hockey is on the verge of big changes. Whether it likes it or not.

PART 2: STEPHEN PEAT

CHAPTER 6
THE HEAVYWEIGHT AND THE BURNING HOUSE

Folks, this is one of the best hockey fights we have seen in a long time.
—Stephen Peat vs. P.J. Stock
(Washington Capitals vs. Boston Bruins, January 5, 2002)

BEFORE YOU read this next story, I need you to do something first. Grab your phone or computer, search "Stephen Peat vs. P.J. Stock" on your browser, then settle into your seat and brace yourself.

This isn't just any run-of-the-mill scrap. It is brutal. It is explosive. It is all-out war. Two professional hockey fighters putting their health, short term and long, on the line in the midst of a ho-hum 6–3 regular season NHL hockey game.

Peat versus Stock remains one of the most violent hockey fights of all time. The play-by-play call from Steve Levy and Darren Pang, then working with ABC Sports, sets the scene as the electric crowd lets out a roar you might usually expect to hear ringside at a title bout. It sounds like bloodlust, adrenaline, and disbelief.

"Stock in the Gold, Stephen Peat in the white at centre ice, here at the FleetCenter in Boston," Levy offers initially, apparently transformed into legendary boxing broadcaster Howard Cosell the moment the gloves hit the ice.

"OH MAN!" Pang exclaims, as both combatants throw a wild array of punches.

"Two guys who can throw punches, and they're doing exactly that," Levy intones, managing, for the moment, to maintain a calmer tone than his partner through the onslaught of violence.

"HOLY JUMPIN'!" Pang blurts out, possibly having lost his mind while riding the rising wave of the crowd's guttural lust. The massive roar rising from the stands now sounds more like William

Wallace–inspired war cries in *Braveheart* than you might ever expect to hear at the good old hockey game.

The announcers, awestruck, then choose to communicate their astonishment at the brawl with a full ten seconds of silence.

But after another dozen or so punches, they're back.

"Folks, this is one of the best hockey fights we have seen in a long time. Punch after punch," Levy states proudly. "Gotta be able to take one to give one, and they are."

"Oh my goodness, what a fight that is!" Pang concludes, stating the painfully obvious.

I've watched the video dozens of times, and I still get shivers. I can feel the goosebumps forming at the hairline on the back of my neck as the hurricane of fists flies. As you watch, consider the magnitude of the violence. The sheer speed and force of the blows is stunning. In this thirty-three-second bare-knuckle bout the punches are direct, constant, and relentless. At one point, Peat takes five straight punches to the face. His left knee appears to buckle, but somehow, the Goliath reawakens to deliver a string of brutal blows of his own.

Neither Peat nor Stock seems to have a self-defence reflex in their arsenal as their arms improbably morph into jackhammers. Aside from some pushing and pulling with their non-punching hands, this is a contest of destruction. Fist to face. Fist to face. Fist to face. And so on. And so forth.

And how about that fighting style? The hands fly so fast it's nearly impossible to keep track, but my best count is thirty-six punches thrown by Stephen Peat and thirty-nine by P.J. Stock. That's more than a punch each per second!

To put this in perspective, in 2018, boxing heavyweight champion Anthony Joshua landed only 139 punches in an entire twelve-round fight (a fight he won). And whereas Peat and Stock might've been expected to fight again in the next game, or God forbid, later in the same game, boxers like Joshua might have one or two bouts per year.

Stephen Peat inflicted a lot of pain throughout his hockey career. Pain was his business, and when he was the one doing the thumping, business was good. Peat went blow for blow with some of the most fearsome fighters to ever play the game, including Donald Brashear, Chris Neil, and Wade Belak. And although Peat was a skilled and powerful pugilist, there's not a fighter alive who has squared off with the likes of the aforementioned worst-dudes-to-ever-put-on-skates without taking a good solid licking of their own. The P.J. Stock fight was a perfect and brutal example of that.

There was a time when Stephen Peat brought thousands of screaming hockey fans to their feet simply by dropping his gloves and throwing his fists. Peat had three stints with the National Hockey League's Washington Capitals between 2001 and 2006. He played alongside the very best players in the world. In 130 NHL games, he earned a reputation as a fighter, with 234 penalty minutes and just ten points. He was charged with protecting some of the most talented players in the game, like 500-goal-scorer Peter Bondra, Hockey Hall of Famer Adam Oates, and two future hall of fame shoo-ins and all-time greats, Jaromír Jágr and Alexander Ovechkin.

Stephen Peat only knew one way to fight. All out, with everything he had. To win. Landing dozens of thunderous blows and receiving equal or greater punishment in kind. And he did it hundreds of times throughout his hockey career. Knowing what we know now about concussions and CTE, it's little wonder he's facing many challenges, living a hellish existence in an ongoing mental health crisis, experiencing on-and-off estrangement from his family, bouts of homelessness, intermittent jail time, and continuing trouble with the law.

Now, with Peat's playing days far behind him, the pain he once handed out so abundantly is his and only his to bear. A man once celebrated by hordes of fans for his ability to bring other mammoth athletes to their knees by sheer violence and force of will is now alone, and facing an uncertain and frightening future.

I first started following Stephen Peat's story closely back in June 2016, after *New York Times* journalist John Branch wrote a feature about him and his dad. I quickly reached out to Stephen's father, Walter Peat, to see if he wanted to share his story on the CBC Radio program *On the Coast*.

His answer was a straightforward no. Walter felt as though he had already made himself vulnerable enough. I got the feeling that he was also pleased with the scope and reach of an article printed in one of the world's most widely read and respected publications.

But because I had watched Stephen growing up (he was a fifteen-year-old defenseman for the Langley Thunder in the BCHL when I was an awkward thirteen-year-old going to the games at the Civic Centre on Friday nights), and because I showed a sustained interest, Walter and I became comfortable with one another. He would promptly return my texts and emails but didn't seem ready to do a live on-air interview. We stayed in touch.

When, nearly a year and a half later, the *New York Times* published a series of Walter's text messages to Branch, I realized it was time to turn up the heat and deliver his part of the story to our local Canadian audience.

After a bunch of back-and-forth, Walter agreed to have me visit his home in Surrey, BC, for an interview. He stipulated that it must be only me and my tape recorder, no videographers or photographers.

When I arrived at the home he shared with his girlfriend, now wife, Jackie, Walter was warm and welcoming. The corpulent sixty-seven-year-old head saw filer at a local sawmill had a full mane of grey and silver hair and walked with a bit of a limp. We settled in at the dining room table, bantering over the dull roar of a Wednesday night NHL game droning somehow appropriately in the background.

Walter wore a crimson Washington Capitals golf shirt with the word "ALUMNI" stitched beneath the logo on his chest. I found the choice of wardrobe a bit confusing considering we were about to dive into a frank and protracted discussion about the pain his son had endured, at least in part, because of his time in the NHL. The conversation would include harsh criticism of the league, and the Capitals in particular. Walter owned this shirt he was wearing *because* of Stephen's pain and suffering.

According to Walter, Stephen, along with his older brother and two sisters, lived a pretty regular life growing up on acreage just outside the small highway stop of a town known as Princeton, BC (population 2,828).

Walter said Stephen was a typical kid, who loved to play with his toys and his bikes. And when hockey was introduced to him at an early age, things seemed to click.

"We had a little rink outside, typical family, you know," Walter reminisced. "[The brothers] used to bruise up their mom's shins pretty good with a hockey puck, and [Stephen] was just always the type of a person that whatever he did, he was good at it."

Not only did Stephen show some exceptional aptitude for the game at a young age, but he soon discovered something that would blow his five-year-old mind. The big guys who were flashing across his TV screen on *Hockey Night in Canada*—they were paid to skate and shoot and score.

"I remember one time we were sitting there watching the hockey game," Walter stated with a smirk on his face. "And he was quite excited by the fact that he had found out that the fellas that were on TV ... were paid to play hockey. He says, 'You know, Dad, I'm going to do that one day.'"

Being from Langley, where the Peats would eventually reside, I know plenty of people who say Walter pushed his boys very hard to succeed in hockey. I've also been told by those same people, and Stephen himself, that Peat learned and internalized from an early age that being good at hockey was the best way of getting his dad's attention.

But when I asked Walter if he could remember the first time he noticed that Stephen was pretty darn good out on the ice, he sent just the opposite message. "I don't know if I really looked at it that way," he said. "I was more concerned about my kids having fun playing hockey and having a special time to play a game that I loved and they loved."

Whether it was Stephen's God-given ability and ferocious determination or heavy-handed pressure from his old man (maybe all of the above), he was quickly becoming one hell of a hockey player. He could skate, he could pass, he could shoot. Stephen was big and exceptionally strong. And it didn't hurt that he hit his growth spurt early, eventually measuring in at six-three and 230 pounds.

At fifteen, Stephen debuted for the BCHL's Langley Thunder. Before long, because of his size, and because he had already shown a fearlessness and a willingness to drop the gloves with players as many as five years older than him, the big defenseman was off to the major junior WHL.

And that's where some of his dad's regrets come in.

"He had good coaching in Langley as a fifteen-year-old, and when he went to the Western Hockey League, of course he's going to be challenged because of his size and stuff, and knowing him, he stood up for himself," Walter said. "For a kid to leave home, I just don't agree with that at all. And I wish I could have kept him at home, because if he would have stayed in Langley, he would have been a lot better going down the road. Maybe he would have stayed here and maybe got a scholarship and get some education and things like that. And maybe have more fun playing again."

When Walter talked about the fun of playing, he meant that in the BCHL, sure, Stephen's toughness was well regarded by coaches, teammates, and fans, it always had been, but he was valued for his hockey skill set too. For his booming shot and his ability to move the puck out of his own zone. For his skating and for his vision. All that changed when he began his career in the WHL with the Red Deer Rebels. The expectation was that Stephen would be an intimidator. He was there to punish his opponents, whether that be with bone-crushing bodychecks or bare-knuckle brawls.

To put that transformation into perspective, Stephen scored twenty points in fifty-nine games in the BCHL at the age of fifteen, an impressive stat for a player that age. In the WHL, Peat would never score twenty points in a season, and amassed only eleven goals and forty-two assists during his entire four-year, 203-game major junior career.

But even if some of the fun had been sapped from the game, the shift from a skilled approach to the enforcer role worked out well for Stephen's career. It rewarded him in the form of a ticket to the big show. The hulking defenseman was selected in the second round, thirty-second overall, by the Anaheim Mighty Ducks in the 1998 NHL entry draft. (Walter points out that out of tens of thousands of kids, Stephen was the only BC hockey player born in 1980 to be drafted into the NHL.) Stephen was about to be paid, and paid handsomely, to play the game he loved, just like the big guys he watched on TV back in his hometown, all those years ago.

The Mighty Ducks traded Stephen's rights to the Washington

Capitals during the 2000 NHL draft, and he began his professional career bouncing back and forth between the Caps and its AHL affiliate, the Portland Pirates. He had been converted from a defenseman to a left winger and was relying evermore on his fists to make his mark on the game. His longest stretch in the NHL came between 2002 and 2004, when he played ninety-one games for the Capitals.

With the momentum of more than a full consecutive NHL season under his belt, Stephen was heading into the 2004–05 season with a lot of confidence. He had gone toe to toe with the toughest players in the NHL and, so far, survived. The money was good too, with Peat raking in about US$500,000 per year.

But before that next season could begin, it was over. During collective bargaining negotiations, the NHL argued that player salaries were out of control, making up too large a proportion of the teams' gross revenues. Commissioner Gary Bettman was demanding a salary cap, something the NHL Players' Association (NHLPA) had vowed never to accept. The boardroom haggling continued for months, significantly delaying the beginning of the season.

Finally, on February 16, 2005, the NHL took the unprecedented step of cancelling the season. It was the first time in eighty-six years the Stanley Cup would not be awarded. (The 1919 Stanley Cup was not awarded because the entire Montreal Canadiens team was infected with influenza!)

Stephen Peat probably didn't know it at the time, but the lockout was the beginning of the end for his pro hockey career. In fact, over the following two seasons, he would play only one more game with the Capitals and nine more games in the AHL. Washington traded him to Carolina in December 2005, but he would never suit up for the Hurricanes. A broken hand, along with injuries to his neck and pelvis, had rendered him ineffective and unable to deliver and withstand pain at the same level he had been accustomed to. Stephen packed up his life in the NHL and returned home to Langley.

Walter Peat said he started noticing big changes in his son shortly after his playing career ended. He said Stephen almost completely lost the ability to focus, which was out of character for a man known to have the patience to rebuild a motorcycle engine on his own. "I remember even when he was playing and his first year getting out of the NHL, he would sit there ... and he had a great temperament for fixing a motorbike," Walter said. "He could take a bike apart. You had to be very delicate with it, and a lot of guys would get mad. Like his older brother would be cussing and swearing, whereas Stephen would just meticulously sit there and take it apart. And he wouldn't break parts. He had such a good temper for that, you know?"

But Stephen's former fastidiousness was one of the first of his defining characteristics to go. Walter said it got so bad that his son would walk into a room for a drink of water and wonder why he had ended up there in the first place. That bewilderment and lack of focus concerned Stephen's father. "It was his forgetfulness, his deterioration in his mindset," Walter said. "It slowly changed to the point where right now he's just a very different person. There's times when he is the old Stephen, happy-go-lucky. But then he seems to kind of go into a phase where he's not there, forgets things. His thought process is scatterbrained. He's all over the place."

In addition to the difficulty focusing, Stephen has told me that he suffers from relentless headaches, memory loss, emotional outbursts, and substance use issues. He hears voices, too. These are all symptoms common with CTE.

Since leaving the NHL, Stephen has had a multitude of legal issues, including accusations of theft, possession of stolen property, resisting or obstructing a peace officer, uttering threats, breaching the terms of his probation, and, perhaps unsurprisingly, trouble stemming from fights at the bar and on the street. Old habits die hard. He's also been the subject of multiple court protection orders from his dad and other members of the family who have claimed that Stephen threatened them in the midst of one of his angry outbursts.

Peat's legal troubles started with a fire at his family house in Langley on March 17, 2015. Authorities deemed it arson and identified Stephen as the main suspect.

According to Peat and his father, the fire was an accident. But that didn't make it any less devastating. Stephen's mother had passed away only about a year before, when her liver failed after years of living with cancer. A hollow feeling of tragedy and loss already hung awkwardly in the air between father and son. Now, with their home in ashes, their relationship was about to get much worse.

Stephen's mother's death wasn't the first rift to emerge in the Peat family. There were wounds that had lingered for years, going all the way back to childhood. But her sudden death reopened those wounds. And the fresh hurt from the house fire revealed those surface wounds to be much deeper. These were gashes.

The Peat family version of the story is that Stephen was using a blowtorch to work on some stereo equipment in the garage (apparently, there was no soldering iron handy). Stephen says the house, which was quite big and relatively new, was purchased for $295,000 with some of his NHL earnings (he says he put $75,000 down). He took great pride in his home.

Because of his brain injuries, Stephen had become highly distractible and forgetful. And that forgetfulness led to a devastating mistake. Stephen said that after receiving a phone call, he walked away from his work, with the blowtorch still lit. Before long, the house was engulfed in flames, and there was an explosion, possibly from an ATV parked in the garage. In Stephen's version of the story, he ran upstairs to the second floor to wake up his dad, ushering Walter and the family dog to safety. Walter does not remember seeing Stephen amid the chaos, saying the explosion is what alerted him to the need to escape.

"Human nature says you're mad, you're upset about it," said Walter Peat. "But the reality of it is he loved working on vehicles, cars, speakers, and stuff, but again, he was at a state ... where he gets distracted so easily, and I would constantly be on him and sometimes frustrated that he wouldn't remember to do things. He was out there working and he was brazing some wires and he gets a phone call. And he forgets that the torch is on the bench on fire ... like it's lit and he [got] distracted."

Walter and Stephen's stories, which are mostly in alignment, differ from the one presented by the local Royal Canadian Mounted Police. In a press release, Langley RCMP corporal Holly Marks said police had determined there was a dispute at the home between a father and son earlier in the day.

According to police, later that evening, after Walter had gone to bed, a person walking by spotted someone trying to start a fire outside the home. "A passerby witnessed the arsonist as he was lighting the fire and made attempts to thwart his efforts," read a statement released by the RCMP. "However, the house fire was reported a short time later."

Stephen and Walter Peat both continue to deny the police account, even years after the event. Walter said Stephen had just returned home from a trip to Prince George, BC. He knew Stephen was back at the house because his son had barged into his room at around 10:30 p.m. to give him a CD he had purchased at a gas station along the way. In Walter's eyes, a simple disagreement between father and son over a rejected late-night gift and an early wake-up time was blown completely out of proportion to the point where the RCMP were using it as a motive for Stephen having allegedly, and maliciously, set the house on fire.

"It was never an argument," Walter remembered. "He got back from Prince George and he brought me a CD—I think it was Alan Jackson—and I said, 'Look, this is not the time to give it to me.' It's ten at night, and I got up at four thirty in the morning. He got frustrated and wanted me to pay attention to him, type of thing."

Stephen turned himself in to police two days after the blaze. Initially, he was charged with arson in relation to an inhabited property and arson damaging property. He pleaded not guilty to both charges, maintaining that the fire was an accident. Six months later, in September 2015, Peat pleaded guilty to the lesser charge of arson by negligence. He was sentenced to one year of probation.

The legal process was over for the time being, which was a relief for Stephen and his dad. But they still had to rebuild the house from the ground up.

"The sad thing is that because of his distraction and inability to focus, he lost the fact that the house was on fire," Walter said. "And when it was on fire it was out of control. It was pretty disheartening to see that because basically a lot of our memories and everything were in the garage. We lost everything. It was pretty upsetting, and I know he's upset about it."

And it wasn't just the brain injuries that were making it difficult for Stephen to focus. As his dad put it, he had started "self-medicating" with drugs to cope with the constant headaches he suffered. In the initial *NYT* article, Stephen admitted to using painkillers, cocaine, and alcohol. Shortly after the fire, Stephen was sent for a rehabilitation stint at the Edgewood Treatment Centre in Nanaimo, on Vancouver Island, BC.

Walter and Stephen were placed under a no-contact order because of ongoing strife and Walter's perception that he was in danger from Stephen. They didn't communicate for a long stretch after the fire. This was highly unusual for a father and son who had been in near-constant communication for Stephen's entire life.

But after about ten weeks at Edgewood, Stephen, who was still suffering from headaches and other symptoms common with CTE, became overwhelmed by the pain and left treatment.

"They wouldn't supply him with any drugs or anything to deal with his headache problems," his father said. "He kept asking, 'Can you give me something to deal with the headaches?' and they would say they'd send him to a specialist, but it never did happen. So one day he got mad and walked out."

It wasn't Stephen's first time in rehab, either. Just like his enforcer colleague James McEwan, Peat took the 2011 deaths of Derek Boogaard, Rick Rypien, and Wade Belak to heart. Their loss led to some self-reflection that pushed him toward an attempt at rehab through the substance abuse and behavioural health program that is run by the NHLPA and the NHL itself. However, the improvement of Peat's mental health outlook was only temporary. Stephen also received some funding from the NHL's Players' Emergency Assistance Fund for a few months to help with his bills while he tried to address his health. But again, the addiction, the headaches, the memory loss, and the outbursts persisted.

Although the fire at the Peat family home didn't result in any jail time for Stephen, it provided a powerful (and literal) smoke signal warning of the legal, addiction, and mental health problems that were only getting worse. The chaos surrounding Stephen Peat was mounting, and this time, he wasn't going to be able to punch his way out of the problem.

Walter remembered one encounter with Stephen that he said became particularly intense in October 2016, a year and a half after the fire. "He got pretty physical with me, and I just thought, 'Well, this isn't going to happen,'" Walter recalled. "He apologized and said he was sorry ... so the thing is, their conscience is there, but [there's] that rage of thinking they're involved with a game."

When I met him on that crisp autumn night at his home in Surrey, Walter said he hadn't spoken to his son in a few days because they were in the midst of one of the court protection orders. Although according to Stephen (and Walter didn't try too hard to hide it), they were still communicating. But the conversations were seldom pleasant and most often combative, bordering on explosive.

"My relationship with my son has gone south," Walter told me. "I still love him, and I'm sure he still loves me, but the point is that I have to look after myself. If you combine ... his frustration of dealing with the headaches and then throw in self-medicating together, that's a recipe for disaster."

Walter mentioned on numerous occasions throughout our conversation that the movie *Concussion* opened his eyes to the reality of CTE and the human fallout it can leave behind. One particularly dramatic moment in the film seemed to have stuck in his mind. In that scene, former Pittsburgh Steelers offensive tackle Justin Strzelczyk is depicted in a violent rage, smashing his belongings and confronting his wife. He says the voices in his head are telling him to kill her. She screams for mercy and orders him to leave. He scrambles to his truck, slams the door, hastily turns the key in the ignition, and speeds off. His wife is in hysterics, screaming at him as he drives away.

Strzelczyk would later die by driving his vehicle 140 kilometres (87 miles) per hour into oncoming traffic on an Upstate New York highway, where he eventually collided with a tanker truck. Somehow, the truck driver sustained only minor injuries.

In repeatedly referring to this particular scene, Walter seemed to be telling me that he was concerned Stephen might suffer a similar fate. I asked him if he's afraid his son will take his own life.

"He gets frustrated and he gets upset and he says, 'I'm going to go kill myself,'" Walter Peat recounted quietly. "It's people breaking down mentally. [They] can't handle it anymore. You lose sleep over it. You get thinking about it and you think, 'Well, tomorrow is going to be the day,' you know? Sometimes I don't know if you kind of just get used to it."

Even though, at that point, Walter's contact with Stephen was intermittent, he said he still heard reports from people who saw his son around and were concerned for him. Sometimes those reports were disturbing.

"The other day I got a call from a friend of Stephen's," Walter said. "He told me that he heard Stephen was in downtown Langley, walking around covered with blood, his hands down around his ankles. When I first heard that I thought, 'Holy shit, man, someone's either beat him up or he's close to dead,' and my heart sunk. But I do realize at some point in time this nightmare is going to end one way or the other. Either he's going to get fixed or he's going to die. I don't want him to be another statistic like Boogaard, or Belak, or Probert, or Rypien. All good young kids."

I've quoted Walter Peat a lot in this chapter. Usually, I would hesitate to tell this much of a person's story from another person's perspective. But because of Stephen Peat's mental and emotional state at the time, and the difficulty connecting with him in person, it was hard not to lean on his dad's side of the story, at least at the beginning.

But despite my ongoing struggles to track Stephen Peat down, I stubbornly convinced myself that a meeting would eventually happen. And I worked relentlessly to make it so.

CHAPTER 7

HOMELESS AND HURTING

The gloves come down for Brashear, and Peat ... There's the left of
Brashear catching Peaty to start this fisticuffs ... I'm not sure if I've
ever seen Brashear lose a fight. He is awfully good, and so is Peat ...
Brashear coming on ... Steve Peat is one game customer, and he and
Donald Brashear legit heavyweights in this league.
—Stephen Peat vs. Donald Brashear
(Washington Capitals vs. Philadelphia Flyers, November 9, 2002)

DESPITE FOLLOWING Stephen Peat's story for more than a year, and publishing two articles about him that had been read by an audience of close to 1 million, I still hadn't spoken with the man himself. We had exchanged dozens of text messages, but he wouldn't answer my calls, and I had never been able to connect with him in person.

It certainly wasn't for lack of effort. I called and texted Stephen almost daily and even spent a day walking around downtown Langley, stopping by places I knew he frequented. I showed nearly everyone I saw his Facebook profile picture on my phone and asked if they recognized him and might know where to find him. A number of people said they knew the face but weren't sure where to look. The bouncer at the local casino recognized him, but "maybe from our clubbing days," he said. I stopped by Stephen's storage space and even knocked on the door at his last known address. No luck.

On one of Stephen's court dates, I went to the provincial courthouse in Port Coquitlam, BC, and waited for him for three hours. I was convinced I'd meet him that day. I could taste it. But Stephen failed to appear. I felt like I was chasing a ghost. A ghost who answered text messages from time to time.

Most days, I would text and call Stephen around seven or eight in the morning, trying to arrange a meeting that day during my shift at CBC Radio. Most often, I'd get nothing back. But maybe once or twice a week, he'd respond around four or five in the afternoon and agree to meet me. (I quickly realized my early-morning attempts were going nowhere. Stephen's a late riser.)

When he did respond, it was usually cordially, if with some reservation and defensiveness. As soon as he'd text me, I would text back and then call. Stephen would never answer the phone. He ignored all my efforts to set a date or time to meet. He never once gave me his actual location. This happened repeatedly, day after day, week after week.

After months of failed attempts, not only was I feeling like a failure of an investigative journalist, but it had also become clear that Stephen either didn't want to meet or, because of his head injuries, and possibly his addiction issues, didn't have the capability or wherewithal to organize it. It was probably a bit of both. I had an idea of the enormity of his struggles. Taking time out to chat with a journalist was probably pretty far down his list of priorities.

The one-sided chase between Stephen and me finally ended on a chilly Friday evening in January 2018. Stephen surprised me with a phone call at around five o'clock while I was at work at the CBC office in Vancouver. Stephen was fired up and ready to vent.

Out of sheer muscle memory, I told him, "Let me call you right back from a studio so I can record our conversation." (This is something I do pretty much every day as part of my job.)

He agreed and hung up.

Immediately, my face flushed and my stomach sank as I realized I might never get him back on the line. Never hang up on your elusive source! I might have squandered my one opportunity to speak with the guy I'd been pursuing and writing about for months. It was an absolute rookie move.

I scrambled into the closest recording booth and quickly dialled his number. I was met with a familiar result. No answer. Straight to voice mail, and the mailbox was full. Oh God, no. The nightmare was real. I felt sick. I rubbed my eyes with both hands and exhaled cartoonishly, preparing for the onslaught of self-hate. *How could I be so stupid?*

I frantically called the number again. Still no answer.

I dialled a third time, already coming to terms with the fact that I'd missed my chance.

Mercifully, Stephen picked up.

Stephen Peat was calling from his truck, which then doubled as his home and sleeping quarters most days and nights. The door was ajar. The rhythmic pulse of the door chime droned ominously in the background as Peat fought through his discomfort to share some of his story.

Stephen was angry. He spoke quickly but lucidly, pausing occasionally to gather himself and fight through the pain.

"My head feels like it's gonna fall off, right now," Peat told me in a strained and intermittently mumbled voice. We were less than a minute into the conversation. His pain hung awkwardly in the air between us. "But I'm doing all right. I mean, what can I do? Hopefully not die."

Peat told me that although he usually lives with headaches, confusion, mental illness, and exhaustion from his brain injuries (symptoms common with CTE), his suffering was much worse than normal. He said he had an infection that seemed to be creeping quickly up the back of his head. He had bumped it on something, but he couldn't seem to remember what. Peat had a prescription to treat the infection but no money to fill it. According to Stephen, things would have been a lot better if his dad would just give him some money. This would prove to be a recurring theme.

No matter whose fault it was, the pain was visceral. I could practically feel it through the phone as his speech rose and fell, grinding like the gears of a machine suddenly losing momentum. I tried my best to let the silence breathe. To ensure he knew there was no pressure.

"Sorry, my head is just hurting right now," he said, almost in a whisper. "I don't even know if I'm going to fuckin' live to finish this fuckin' story the way it feels right now."

I asked Stephen if he could describe the pain for me.

"I can't even describe it right now," he responded. "It just feels like the top of my head is going to fuckin' blow off, and it literally is ... like something's wrong."

As Stephen talked through his pain and found a tenuous groove, his speech sped up and his voice began to rise. His thoughts were propelled by anger. He was reaching full-on diatribe, his ire directed at one person and one person only: his dad, Walter.

"Fact is, I can't rent a place because I'm a convicted arsonist with no fuckin' job, and a disability, and no way of guaranteeing that I've got rental money," he said. "My dad has it, he just won't fuckin' give it to me because he thinks I spend too much money."

Walter said Stephen spends too much money, especially on destructive things like drugs and alcohol. Stephen said that isn't true. Stephen's fury was laser focused on Walter because he said his dad didn't share any of the insurance money that came from the sale of the rebuilt house after the fire. But Walter said that isn't true.

"He got reimbursed for everything from that fire," Stephen said. "I think he got around $200,000 cash ... A lot of that stuff in the garage was my stuff, but he got all the money for it, not me. I didn't get a fuckin' penny."

I asked Stephen if he believes he got a raw deal.

"I know I got a raw deal. I got fucked," he stated emphatically. "I got sent off to a rehab facility, after an accidental arson charge. The fuckin' arson investigation has nothing to do with where the fire even started and my dad tells the police he didn't see me there? How do you think he got out of the fuckin' fire? I woke the fuckin' prick up and got him out of the fire. And he doesn't tell the cops that? What is wrong with him?"

Stephen was angry with his dad for taking their story to the media in the first place. Walter said he didn't know what else to do.

"I just want my health back, man," Stephen said as his anger faded. "I don't want this. I don't care about houses. I don't care about money. Fuck, he thinks I spend all this money on drugs and alcohol and he doesn't understand that I'm buying Band-Aids and fucking shit for the back of my head."

Stephen asked himself aloud, or maybe someone else in the truck, if there was a scarf handy that he could wrap around his head to help with the headache. He mumbled something about being really uncomfortable.

One of the most emotional moments of our nearly hour-long conversation was when Stephen talked about his beloved dog. He said that one of the hardest things about being mostly estranged from his dad was that he'd hardly seen his dog. And it hurt. He was fighting back tears.

"I spent every fuckin' day of my life with our dog, Dawson," he said, anguish in his voice. "I spent every fuckin' day, morning to night. This dog slept with me and everything for the last four years. My dad scoops that dog up ... I've seen the dog once since then in a year. Four fucking years with a fucking dog every morning to night, and now I don't even get to see the dog? It's the cruelest thing you can fuckin' do to someone."

As Stephen's tirade eased a bit, I told him that his dad had expressed a great deal of concern for his current situation, and that Walter told me he loses sleep at night thinking about what might happen to him.

Stephen bristled at the suggestion. "He's losing sleep at night?" he repeated incredulously. "Think about this, over Christmas I slept in my car Christmas Eve, Christmas Day, Boxing Day, like five days in a row."

Just when I thought Stephen's rekindled anger might build to a rage, he slammed on the brakes. It was as though the sadness of his Christmas spent alone stopped the anger dead in its tracks. Maybe he was actually more demoralized than angry. His tone softened. The drone of the door chime returned, reclaiming the space vacated by his exasperated voice.

Stephen sounded defeated. "It was the worst Christmas I've ever had," he said quietly. "I spent it alone in my truck. It was awful."

Stephen's pain and sadness overcame him. He told me it was too much and he had to go. He hung up the phone.

Most of us get headaches from time to time. Whether from stress, a loud work environment, or maybe a bad hangover, there's nothing quite like a pounding headache to make a day spent curled in a dark room, hiding from the world, look like the best way to go.

Now imagine the worst headache you've ever had, only it doesn't go away. Not ever. Advil and Tylenol do nothing. Stronger prescription drugs provide some relief but only temporarily. It pounds and pounds, and then pounds some more.

That's the kind of pain that blares across Stephen Peat's brain every day. He told me it's frustrating, discombobulating, and often intolerable. The headaches started a year or so after his NHL playing career ended.

Stephen said they're pretty much constant, throwing his entire existence off-kilter from the moment he awakes in the morning, until the moment he can find rest at night. There were many days when Peat's only refuge was a quiet, dark room where the raging kiln of pain in his head could be reduced to a rolling boil.

Because of these headaches, along with the other symptoms he suffers, like depression, memory loss, addiction, and hearing voices, Stephen can barely get up in the morning for his weekly probation meetings that keep him out of prison. And holding down a job, at this point, has become an unrealistic and unattainable goal. So he relied almost entirely on financial support from his dad. And that could be a complicated proposition, because sometimes Walter turned off the financial taps, leaving Stephen to fend for himself. In some cases when the Walter well ran dry, things got bad.

Stephen Peat was homeless.

This reality is hard to fathom. Stephen Peat, the mighty former fighter, the bringer of pain, tougher than nails and then some, had no place to go. The man who spent his career standing up for teammates (and making nearly $2 million in the process) was now living alone, sleeping in the cab of a beat-up GMC pickup or crashing on the couches of any friend who would have him. He was spending most of his days in local parks, trying to find some relief from the relentless headaches and the fog of confusion that surrounded, then swallowed, his life.

About two weeks after our first surprise phone call, Stephen called me again. Only this time, he sounded like a completely different person. Gone was the wincing and grumbling man who had been brought to his proverbial knees by brutal pain. In his place was a soft-spoken, friendly guy who just seemed keen to chat for a bit. This was the gentle giant I'd heard about from his dad and so many others. It may seem counterintuitive, but hockey enforcers are well known for their kind and sympathetic nature off the ice.

Stephen's tone was warm, and he was quick to laugh. The conversation was comfortable, and he seemed as interested in hearing my perspectives as he was in sharing his own. He was skilled and generous in facilitating our back-and-forth. But polite manner aside, Stephen was still a bit scattered. He was happily surprised when I told him it was Thursday, because he thought it was Friday (this meant he didn't have to visit his parole officer that day). But he had his wits about him enough to be aware of his challenges and have some reasonable working ideas about how he might address them.

As our chat evolved beyond pleasantries, Stephen turned to his most frequent topic of conversation: his dad. Walter had given him money to fill his prescription for the wound on the back of his head. He even had enough money to pay for a couple of nights in a motel. But despite the two-week break, Stephen picked up pretty much where we had left off in our initial conversation.

"[My dad] does this thing where he likes to say his piece and he just hangs up the phone and blocks me so I can't talk to him, right?" Stephen said. "It drives me absolutely fuckin' nuts. Just before the house went up for sale, he's probably had me blocked eighty percent of the time. It's really annoying. What happens is we start slowly getting along, but as soon as one subject arises that he doesn't like, he turns it into ... you know ..."

When Stephen is more lucid, as he was that day, he's acutely aware of his most pressing challenge: finding a safe, warm place to stay. Like so many people who have experienced homelessness, he spends most of his time and energy figuring out where he'll sleep next. And he knows that lacking a consistent residence is holding him back from accomplishing his most pressing tasks.

"Yesterday was just a mess of a day. I didn't get anything accomplished," he told me. "And the worst part is, you can have those days, but add on top of that not having a home base, like living out of your car pretty much. It drives me insane."

Peat's search for a home, badly hampered by his battered brain and lack of employment, is made worse by Metro Vancouver's insanely expensive rental housing market. One-bedroom basement suites in the Langley and Surrey areas rent for between $1,000 and $1,500 per month. And it only goes up from there if you want something nicer. That's tough cash to cover when nearly all of your energy is spent trying to escape a never-ending diabolical headache, not to mention other debilitating symptoms. Like tens of thousands of others in Metro Vancouver, for Stephen, the rent's too high and the income's too low. At that point, he was among the more than 3,600 people in the region living without a home, according to the 2017 Metro Vancouver homeless count.[9]

"I have trouble finding something to rent," he said. "It's either too pricey for a single guy, or it's priced good, but ... I'm not making this kind of money. The other thing is, I'm really reluctant to have roommates, because I've had roommates in the past in hockey and stuff, and I don't have energy or the time to clean up after someone else, and I like my place clean."

In this extended moment of clarity, Stephen even framed some of his challenges in a humorous way. He told me about a truly frightening recurring experience with a playful tone in his voice.

"I wake up some days and the whole house is backwards," Peat said. "It's awful, man. I'm just like, 'Where the fuck is the front door?' Or I wake up and I think I'm in a hotel room, but I'm actually in someone's apartment or something and there's people talking and I'm like, 'Who the fuck?' ... and I've been stuck in a bedroom for like two hours, peeking out the fuckin' door, being like, 'Where am I?' And the worst is I'm not fuckin' hungover or anything. I'm just like, 'This is fuckin' weird.'"

I forced myself to ask the most glaringly obvious and important question, even though it didn't feel right in the moment. Perhaps there just isn't a "right" moment to ask about traumatic head injuries.

Does Stephen think he has CTE?

"I don't know, man, what [it's] from. I think it's from [CTE]," he said. "It was also from stress, just not knowing what the fuck is going on, you know?"

Stephen avoided large-scale reflection or investigation of root causes and instead quickly pivoted to his go-to. The thing that's right in front of his face. One of the last people with a meaningful role in his life. His bread-and-butter grievance for which he blames many, if not all of his problems—his dad.

I spent hours talking to Stephen Peat, and for most of that time, it felt as though he was trying to talk to his father through me. Even when he was lucidly describing his hockey-playing days, his living situation, or maybe a fond childhood memory, we were always one quick turn away from a rant about Walter.

"I feel like I kind of get my dad on a level playing field once in a while," he digressed. "But ever since he kind of gained control ... with all the finances through the house ... Like it used to be my mom had it all, and she passed away and my dad just worked relentlessly to gain control of everything. And then losing the house and me going to rehab, [he] kept gaining more and more leverage. Now, it's like he's power-tripping ... I mean, I don't know if most parents are like this or not, but he does not want to entertain anything aside from what he feels and what he thinks happened."

As the conversation once again shifted away from his preoccupation with his dad, Stephen's tone lightened to match the unusually bright and sunny winter day. He told me that he's not taking drugs aside from his prescriptions. He told me he knows self-medicating is bad for him, and he has turned to naturopathy in the past and hopes to return to it in the future. Stephen said he's been giving veganism a shot but can't afford it right now, joking that Whole Foods should be called Whole Paycheque. He said he's trying to watch his diet and keep his weight down, and eating vegan helps a bit with the headaches. I told him veganism is a great idea, but burgers and pizza taste way too good. We shared a chuckle.

The idea of the two of us getting together came up multiple times throughout the conversation, and Stephen seemed more open to meet than ever before. As the conversation came to a close, I asked him when and where we should meet the following day.

Before he hung up, he told me he had to first check with his parole officer, Heather, and he'd get right back to me. Unsurprisingly, he never did.

CHAPTER 8
VOICES

And now here's Boulton and Peat gonna go at it. Boulton and Peat
drop 'em and they want to be in the centre ring right at centre ice!
Now Peat gets the upper hand and starts swingin' over the top, punch-
ing away at the back of Boulton's head ... Boulton trying to get his arm
free ... OH! ... a right right on the schnoz from Boulton to Peat! Peat
fires one underneath. Boulton comes back with a wild right, and down
on the ice they go!
—Stephen Peat vs. Eric Boulton
(Washington Capitals vs. Buffalo Sabres, November 26, 2003)

THE FEBRUARY 2018 CBC article I wrote after finally speaking with Stephen Peat exploded across the country. It was read more than 750,000 times the first day it was published. When a story receives that kind of traffic it gets left near the top of the main CBC national news page, and from there, hit begets hit begets hit. It was even the top story on Apple's suggested news on the iPhone for a few hours that day. Peat's story resonated with Canadians and took on a life of its own.

Not long after the article was published, I started receiving phone calls and emails from complete strangers. I got an email from a therapist in Ontario offering Stephen a spot at his rehab centre free of charge. He told me Stephen could come anytime. A man in London, Ontario, whose family had billeted junior players wanted me to know he would be willing to have Stephen move in. He even offered him a construction job upon arrival. I got a tweet from Sarena Snider, the daughter of former Philadelphia Flyers owner Ed Snider, offering to help enroll Stephen in a program called Athletes for CARE that advocates for hockey players after their careers are over. I received a call from a man saying he was Stephen's ex-girlfriend's brother.

Apparently, Stephen had given him a signed and framed jersey of all-star goaltender and former Washington Capitals teammate Olaf Kölzig. He wanted to give it back. They had never been close friends, but Stephen's kindness had touched him, and now, with Stephen's back against the wall, he wanted to return the favour.

The response was overwhelming.

But it wasn't coming only from random, kind-hearted hockey fans across the continent. I heard from enforcers too. Former Philadelphia Flyer Riley Cote and former New York Ranger Dale Purinton, and even James McEwan said they wanted to help. They wanted to know if I was in contact with Stephen. Maybe they could come with me to talk with him and nudge him toward the help he needed. If that wasn't possible, they simply wanted to send Peat a message of kindness in his time of struggle.

"He's not alone and there's a huge group of people who would love to offer him support," Riley Cote told me from his home in Pennsylvania. "There's hope for everyone. He's in a dark place right now, and there are people around who are willing to help him get out of this funk."

James McEwan was one of the first former enforcers to reach out. Having faced the demons of a post-fighting career, and shared his struggles publicly through the CBC, he follows these kinds of stories closely. He started texting me only hours after the Peat article was published. I learned later that McEwan contacted Stephen's dad as well, which Walter told me he appreciated.

When we spoke on the phone, James was concerned but optimistic. "My message to him is that healing is possible, and no matter how tough things are right now, it is possible to bounce back and to come out of this," McEwan said confidently. "He can heal and become balanced and strong again."

Dale Purinton went toe to toe with Stephen Peat on more than a few occasions. Peat and Purinton crossed paths in the WHL and fought multiple times in the NHL. But with Stephen Peat facing a very different kind of fight, his former foe wanted to help.

Purinton spoke calmly and with purpose over the phone, as though he were speaking to Peat himself. More than anything, he spoke like someone who understands. "I support him and I'm here for him and I can't give advice," said Purinton. "I just have to be open to listen to him. I got his back and I just want to see him get well."

The parallels between Peat and Purinton go beyond hockey. Purinton visited Peat at the Edgewood Treatment Centre on Vancouver Island after the house fire in 2015. Only about a year later, Purinton was attending that very centre to address problems of his own. Their connection is born from a common experience of facing the very real difficulties that stem from life as a hockey enforcer.

"You're kind of playing out your dreams in a way, but what are you giving up for that?" Purinton asked rhetorically, the answer painfully obvious. "Unfortunately, some people are giving up their lives and their health ... [Former enforcers] can relate to the sadness, and to the darkness."

Purinton told me that he could help Peat find the funding to go into treatment, but that Stephen would have to want to go. This wasn't the first or last time I heard this condition in reference to Stephen and his issues with addiction. He has to *want* to go. At that point, the "want" had been one of the key missing pieces. Even when Peat had agreed to seek out rehabilitation services, the "want" had worn out, and quickly. Stephen had always left well before he'd completed the necessary work to achieve a lasting sobriety.

With his challenges out in the open, Peat's fellow warriors were showing that they were there to help. But what about the National

Hockey League? Having heard the concern from fans, colleagues, and complete strangers, you might be wondering what Stephen's former employer thought about his story. While researching and writing the article, I sent dozens of emails and called the NHL head office in New York dozens of times more. After weeks of this, I had not received a single response.

But just before the story was set to roll out on CBC.ca, I received a statement from John Dellapina, the league's vice-president of communications. It did not address Stephen's situation, citing privacy concerns.

"As you probably know, among the most important pillars of our various player assistance programs are anonymity and confidentiality," Dellapina wrote. "Except in specific cases that result in suspensions to active players, the League neither announces if or when players enter any of our programs or receive any assistance nor do we acknowledge that they have. It is that anonymity and confidentiality that enables players to seek help without fear of either unwanted publicity or any potential hindrance to future opportunities. For that reason, we can't and won't comment."

After the CBC article, Stephen Peat was once again at the centre of the hockey world, at least for a day or two. Despite his challenging, desperate, and lonely situation, it had become clear that people from inside the hockey world and out sincerely care about him. To see that visceral outpouring of support was certainly heartening, if not necessarily helpful to Peat in the long run. And the questions remained: Was he capable of seeking out and receiving that help? And did he even want it in the first place?

As a journalist, I wasn't sure what to do with all the messages, kindnesses, and offers of help. I reflected upon an old adage repeated to me by older journalists: "It's not your job to save them; it's just your job to tell their story."

And while that piece of conventional wisdom is true in many scenarios, I felt that I couldn't take such a detached approach with Stephen. Whether I liked it or not, I had become a point of contact, even an intermediary, in the eyes of many who had read the article.

My solution was to play the role I know best: reporter. I relayed succinct versions of the messages to Stephen by text in the hope that, at best, he might take someone up on one of their kind offers to help. At worst, it might simply make him feel good to know people care about him. I forwarded dozens of these messages to Stephen. He never once responded.

I had spoken with Stephen Peat on the phone a couple of times, but meeting up proved to be exceedingly difficult. I tried and I tried and I tried again, for more than a year. At some points it felt surreal and almost Kafkaesque.

Here's an example of a days-long text message exchange with Stephen Peat:

Monday, January 22, 2018, at 12:42 p.m.
Jeremy: Hi Stephen. I hope you had a good weekend. Just checking in to see if you want to talk sometime. I can come to you if it's easier.
2:28 p.m.
Stephen: Sure. Tomo work?
2:29 p.m.
Jeremy: Yeah, that works. What time and where?
2:31 p.m.
Stephen: Will let u kniw later
2:32 p.m.
Jeremy: Ok. Sounds good.

(End of day)

Tuesday, January 23, 2018, at 10:30 a.m.

Jeremy: Hey. What's a good time to meet today?

10:48 a.m.

Stephen: Not sure. I am feeling upset all morning. What time works for u. Just hoppibg in shower.

10:52 a.m.

Jeremy: I am available most of the day. I don't want to rush you if you're not feeling well. But if you feel better in a bit, we could meet. Why don't you shower and chill for a bit and let me know how you feel in an hour or two ...

1:22 p.m.

Jeremy: Feelin any better?

(End of day)

Wednesday, January 24, 2018, at 9:20 a.m.

Jeremy: Hey Stephen. How are you doin today. Any better?

5:57 p.m.

Stephen: Wanna schedule for in the morn. Feel way bettrr.

6:14 p.m.

Jeremy: Sure. 10?

(End of day)

Thursday, January 25, 2018, at 9:07 a.m.

Jeremy: How're you feeling today?

12:42 p.m.

Jeremy: How's it goin?

4:02 p.m.

Stephen: Good. Can u do tonight

4:10 p.m.

Jeremy: Shit. I can't sorry man. Tomorrow pretty much anytime.

(End of day)

Friday, January 26, 2018, at 9:30 a.m.

Jeremy: Hey man. How's your day lookin?

(End of day)

This kind of disjointed communication would continue even when Stephen was the one reaching out to me.

Monday, February 26, 2018, at 3:10 p.m.

Stephen: Hey. How r u today

3:10 p.m.

Jeremy: Not bad. How are you?

3:11 p.m.

Stephen: Hanging in there. I will be able to talk in hour.

3:11 p.m.

Jeremy: You goin to court tomorrow?

(End of day)

Tuesday, February 27, 2018, at 3:26 p.m.

Jeremy: How was court?

(End of day)

These kinds of texts, and attempted phone calls, continued for months. It was almost funny in its absurdity, except that it felt really serious too. Bizarre might be a better way of putting it. There were many moments when I was almost certain that we would never meet. But I kept trying.

On May 30, 2018, my messages stopped going through. I got that little red exclamation mark on the right side of the screen with "Not Delivered" underneath.

It turned out Stephen had been sent to prison. He had been arrested and charged with assaulting a peace officer and wilfully resisting or obstructing a peace officer. Via text, his dad told me that Stephen caused a scene at a tow yard in Surrey. His truck was inside and he wanted it back but wasn't allowed to get it. It sounded as though Stephen lost his cool. The police were called, an altercation occurred, and he was taken into custody.

After nearly two months, he started answering my texts again. But it was more of the same. A seeming eagerness to meet followed by a dearth of details, and ultimately, no meeting. At first, I thought he was toying with me. That he didn't actually want to meet up. But now I've become convinced that it wasn't intentional. I'm convinced, too, that fluid and coherent communication via text or phone is simply something Stephen Peat was not equipped to handle at that time.

For example:

> *August 29, 2018, at 11:05 a.m.*
>
> Jeremy: What's going on, man?
>
> (End of day)
>
> *August 30, 2018, at 12:33 p.m.*
>
> Stephen: What you mean
>
> *12:35 p.m.*
>
> Jeremy: How are you?
>
> *12:36 p.m.*
>
> Jeremy: Where are you? We could go for lunch.
>
> *12:37 p.m.*
>
> Stephen: Yes
>
> Jeremy: I'll meet you
>
> *12:38 p.m.*
>
> Stephen: Ok.
>
> *12:41 p.m.*
>
> Jeremy: Where you at? I'm hungry (pizza emoji, pizza emoji)
>
> *4:16 p.m.*
>
> Jeremy: Want to meet up tomorrow? I'm free all day
>
> (End of day)

But on August 31, 2018, after all those months of trying to meet up, something different happened. For the first time ever, Stephen gave me his location:

> *August 31, 2018, at 9:59 a.m.*
> Jeremy: Can meet whenever wherever
> *11:38 a.m.*
> Stephen: Hey
> Jeremy: What's up
> *11:39 a.m.*
> Stephen: Am around
> Jeremy: Where are ya?
> *11:43 a.m.*
> Stephen: Port wells.
> Jeremy: Ok. On my way.
> *11:44 a.m.*
> Jeremy: Port Kells, right?
> *11:51 a.m.*
> Stephen: Yes. Just at Alderauto
> *11:52 a.m.*
> Jeremy: See ya shortly

I immediately rushed out the door and drove from Vancouver to Surrey (about thirty-five kilometres, twenty-two miles, southeast). I tried not to speed, but my right foot felt a bit heavy as I crossed the ten-lane Port Mann Bridge heading into Vancouver's biggest suburb.

I arrived at Alder Auto, a mechanic shop with an extensive auto parts store attached, and tried to appear nonchalant as I walked up and down the cluttered aisles looking for Stephen. There was still a part of me that expected him not to be there. He wasn't inside, and I didn't see his truck. I stood in the parking lot and pulled out my phone to see if I could track him down.

But sure enough, just as I unlocked the screen, Stephen emerged from a side door and walked over to shake my hand. He was wearing blue jeans, a plain white T-shirt, and a backwards white hat perched atop his head that read, *Petro-Canada Lubricants*. He was also wearing a white plastic bracelet. He'd recently been in the hospital.

Stephen seemed approachable and calm, if not a bit distant and uneasy. At first, our conversation was stilted. I was asking questions (pleasantries, not hard-hitting journalism), and he was a bit slow to respond. His speech was deliberate, with long pauses. I wasn't sure whether this was thoughtfulness, hesitation, or something else.

With awkwardness swirling in the air between us, I thought we might both be more comfortable seated, so I suggested we get lunch. He mentioned a Tim Hortons just a few blocks away, so we climbed into my car and headed that way.

I found out that Stephen had been in jail for fifty-three days. He said his time in prison wasn't all bad. He praised his lawyer for getting him out earlier than expected. Peat told me he was getting along well with his dad (which hadn't been the case for a very long time), so much so that he was living in an RV in the driveway of Walter's Surrey home.

At the coffee shop, we ordered and sat with our food at a small table in the back corner. This was where things took a disturbing turn.

Based on my knowledge of Stephen's story, I was prepared to encounter a person facing serious challenges. But the reality of the situation was much worse than I anticipated.

After Stephen wolfed down his wrap and downed three-quarters of a large Iced Capp, he started trying to tell me something, but he couldn't quite get the words out.

"I just wanna ..." he trailed off. "I think I just gotta ..."

These slowly forming half thoughts were followed by as much as twenty or thirty seconds of silence. The awkwardness felt precarious. The last thing I wanted to do was push Peat for answers in this state, so I waited for him to gather himself. When he finally gained the composure to speak more than a broken sentence or two, what I found out about his mental health was alarming.

Stephen told me that the reason he had trouble making phone calls, returning texts, and keeping appointments was that he was dealing with "a lot of noise." After a few more minutes, I discovered that the noise he was referring to was actually voices in his head. Stephen said they were constant and perpetually changing. He told me that he often felt like he was on a radio show or in a reality TV show. He thought people were watching him. He believed the RCMP was tracking his every move because of his criminal record. He heard what he believed to be police drones outside his RV at night. The delusions were haunting him at every turn. Stephen said he'd been hearing them for about a year.

I asked him, when he thought he was on a reality TV show, who was watching him.

"I don't know who it is," he said. "That's what I keep trying to seek out: 'Who is this?' I have an idea, though. I keep thinking it's something that I could find out one day. It's frustrating, man."

Stephen broke the tension momentarily with a laugh, shook his head, and then asked me earnestly, "Do you have any ideas about this?"

I considered my words carefully, and then told him that it was probably something in his brain that was making him think and feel that way. I told him it was highly unlikely that someone was watching him or listening to him.

"I wonder if it's something that I could be in control of," he wondered aloud. "Is it something other than inside of me is what bothers me. It's an outside thing. I don't think it's something inside me."

I once again suggested that, probably, it was his brain not working the way it was supposed to.

"That's what I'm confused about, right?" he said. "I just feel like ... I feel like I'm in *The Twilight Zone* or something."

I asked Stephen if he wanted to understand the voices or get rid of them.

"I want to figure it out and get rid of it at the same time," he said. "Sometimes I feel like my privacy is being invaded, and then sometimes it's fun. But sometimes I'm trying to sleep at night and I'm just like, 'Go away.' I feel like I don't know if it's all in my head or not. That's the problem."

I asked him if he had spoken to anyone about the voices. If he'd asked for help.

"I tried to talk to someone about it and I got thrown in the wacky bin," Peat said. "They threw me in the hospital for three days. A couple of weeks ago I was in a psychiatric place. I thought there was someone flying a drone above me. I'm pretty sure it was, yeah, someone was watching me. Problem is, I'm a criminal, right? I've got a criminal record, so I don't know if they're allowed to watch me. Maybe ... (pauses) maybe the RCMP is."

There was another long pause as Stephen appeared to focus on the very voices he'd been describing. "Right now it seems like they're pissed off at me in my head," Peat said. "I'm not entertaining them or something. The voices got really quiet when you came around, though."

Stephen told me the existence of the voices and the effort it took to figure them out had left him exhausted. Then, after some hesitation, he began to let me in on the kind of stuff he was hearing.

"It seems like there's something trying to hurt me," he said. "There's like, good and evil. I don't feel it's necessary to choose one of them, but I'm hearing them both. The thing won't let me go; the voices won't go."

I asked Peat if he shared this information with his dad or his probation officer. He told me that he didn't because it was "just craziness." So in moments, Stephen seemed to understand that the voices were delusions. But most of the time, he found it difficult to differentiate.

"You know what I'm going to do," he began. "I'm going to try to figure ... (big sigh and pause). Fuck. I wish I knew more about what was going on in my head, like I feel like I'm ... (big pause) I don't know."

I told him that delusions and other mental health issues are common symptoms of CTE. I suggested that the best thing to do would be to try to get to the doctor, quickly, and then go on a regular basis.

"I feel like I got some sort of cross-contamination thing going on," Peat said. "Like reality and illusion, but it's making sense, but it's not to me. I've got some crazy thoughts going on, but that's why I definitely don't want to share them."

At that point, I told Stephen that I had the number for Glenn Healy, former NHL goaltender and executive director of the NHL Alumni Association. I communicated that I'd interviewed Glenn and he'd insisted that if any former player needed help, the alumni association would be there for them. I offered to call Healy right then and there. I brought the number up on my phone and showed it to him.

Stephen wanted me to slow down. It was a hard no. And in that moment, he finally seemed to gain some clarity. "I don't want them to send me to some clinic," Peat said. "I like being back with my father and stuff, but I'd really like to talk to someone about what's going on upstairs to help me simmer down the noise, because the noise is too much for me. I'm not thinking for myself right now. I'm thinking about all this racket. I got to quit fighting that and have something more stable and sleep better."

The rest of our conversation was a bit scattered. Stephen asked about one day coming to visit the CBC studios in Vancouver. He told me he'd been to the NHL studios in New York City. We talked about a counsellor in Surrey who is known to work with athletes. Maybe he could help. (I later realized that person is interventionist and addictions counsellor Andy Bhatti, who knows Stephen well.)

After a few more minutes, Stephen had had enough. We left the Tim Hortons, and I dropped him back at his truck in the auto shop parking lot.

We shook hands and he promised to keep in touch. As I prepared to drive back to Vancouver, I glanced over at Stephen sitting in his truck. He had taken off his hat and was rubbing his face with both hands. His deep discomfort was visceral. He looked like a heavyweight boxer who'd found himself lying on the mat but wasn't quite sure how he got there. Exhaustion and defeat were written all over his face.

I left my meeting with Peat contemplating the depth of darkness and loneliness that he was facing. And it made me feel like shit. As I hit the highway, I reflected on the encounter. Although the interview had only lasted about an hour, it was one of the toughest I've ever been through. There were moments that made me deeply uncomfortable, particularly when Stephen was describing the good and evil voices in his head telling him what to do. It doesn't take much of an imagination to go to a bad place with that idea. I wouldn't say that I was scared, though. Peat's demeanour was gentle throughout, but it was clear to me that this was someone who had been in a state of deep mental distress for a long time. That's hard to witness and even harder to reckon with.

Some high-flying mental and emotional acrobatics were required to negotiate the journalistic balancing act I found myself in. I was and am not Stephen's advocate. I believed his story was an important one to tell. But I didn't want to be in it. I was simply trying to observe it and share it in the hope that it might resonate. As the drive came to a close, though, I realized one thing. I had to at least try to lend a hand.

I reached out to Glenn Healy, who had always assured me, on the record and off, that if Stephen wanted help to deal with his addiction problems, he would get it. I told Healy what I'd seen, and he echoed my concern. I realized, however, that this was not a problem that would be solved by Healy and his organization. They had made it clear they're not in the business of rescuing people. They're set up to help players but only when the player wants help. When the player is committed to healing and turning his life around. And Stephen just wasn't there. Not even close.

While I got what Healy was saying, I couldn't help but think that making the "want" a prerequisite for care wasn't all that fair either. Stephen Peat's mental health was in shambles. Yes, at that point, he had a place to live, in the RV in his dad's driveway, but he wasn't well. Far from it. You can say the help is there for those who want it all you like, but this was not someone who possessed the mental and emotional strength to face down rehabilitation. He wasn't in any condition to get to a potentially life-saving appointment or treatment, let alone hold down a job. Christ, it took me eleven months just to meet up with the guy, and we live less than an hour apart. Whether the organizations out there are designed for it or not, this was a person who would require a rescue.

And on the subject of drugs, you might be wondering if Stephen was high when I met with him. At the time, I didn't think so. Because of media reports and discussions with sources, I was looking for signs of someone who might be using cocaine, methamphetamine, or other uppers. But he was mostly relaxed. His eyes weren't dilated, his speech was slow, his jaw calm. No sign of jitters you might link to a drug like coke. I have no clue if Stephen had taken any drugs that day, but it would be naive to think that it wasn't at least a possibility. Ultimately, however, you could pretty easily argue that it's immaterial. Whether he was high or not, this was simply a man who needed help.

I made a couple more calls and sent a handful of text messages to people I thought might be able to help Stephen, but the responses were mostly more of the same: "He has to be ready to get help." As much as I wished he were ready, I would've been lying if I said it was true.

As it turned out, though, someone did make contact with Stephen, only one day after I saw him. Unfortunately, it wasn't the NHL, the NHLPA, or the NHL Alumni Association. It wasn't an addictions counsellor or his parole officer. It wasn't even his dad.

It was the police. Stephen was charged with mischief and not showing up to his parole meeting. He was sent back to prison, again, where he spent another month or so behind bars. With no help in sight for his brain injuries, addictions, and other mental health challenges, his slow and painful transformation from NHL enforcer to man caught in the crossfire of a mental health crisis and the judicial system was all but complete.

Think back to that fight between Stephen Peat and P.J. Stock. The explosiveness. The thunderous violence. The relentless fists and the roaring crowd. Set aside the brutality for just a moment and take a minute to reflect upon the impressive power, the toughness, and the athleticism it takes to survive such a fight. Think about not only the physical supremacy needed to dispense such devastating force but the mental fortitude required to withstand it in equal measure. That fight, however horrifying, is a feat of human strength, endurance, and courage.

Now think about Stephen's fall. Think about where he ended up: on-and-off homeless, in and out of jail, struggling with addiction, and hearing voices. It's hard to believe.

Stephen Peat was a titan out on the ice, but he's a lot more than that too. He was a skilled motorcycle mechanic. He is funny and charismatic and kind. He is a friend. He is a brother and he is a son. But first and foremost, fighter or not, drugs or not, arson or not, homeless or not, jailed or not, he's just a regular guy. And he needs help.

Just as I was putting the final, somewhat depressing, touches on Stephen's story for this book in October of 2018, I received another update. It came first from the addictions counsellor and interventionist Andy Bhatti, and then from Stephen himself.

Stephen told me that he was at a treatment centre in Powell River, on BC's Sunshine Coast, and that he was feeling a lot better. "It's a good spot," he wrote to me in a succinct email. "I think I am getting some decent quiet time. Just wanted to thank you for talking to me."

Bhatti outlined some of the treatments Stephen was receiving, and told me that he and Stephen might call later in the week. But the call never came, and I didn't follow up. That kind of work is better left undisturbed.

Then, one week later, Stephen posted a thoughtful and mostly coherent status update on Facebook. That he was able to achieve such clarity is an achievement considering how severe his delusions were only weeks earlier.

Because I have written so much about Stephen but with limited interviews to draw from, I have included the whole post, unedited.

October 15, 2018, 4:28 p.m.

In 99 I helped my family buy a house. It cost 295000. I assisted by putting up 25 percent down which amounted to 75000. After 17 years it sold for 950000. During those years I had a short career in the nhl. My mother passed away and I have had to deal with problems from injuries that landed me in treatment centers. I spent all I had with therapists on my own and self medication but seem to never have found the magical cure ... the nhl and nhlpa have both helped me. My more recent problems that have raised are mainly due to a family feud between my father and I. I accidentally burned down that house I once helped a financially struggling family acquire. That was years ago. The rcmp charged me with numerous charges which I all didn't agree with but to avoid a costly trial I plead out to a lesser charge. I served 2 years probation. The house was rebuilt and contents replaced in cash. I spent my free time helping when I could. My father and I both agreed to sell once completed. And at this time he agreed to compensate me for my investment. As the house [was] now available I noticed my father changed. He created a dtorsional hate for me. He criticized me and belittled me. The house sold and now he was blocking my calls and sending texts that explained to me how much it cost to raise me and I was not gonna receive a cash sum for my time or investment from the house. Now this is when he turned to John branch of the new York Times. I now since then have spent about 80 days in jail. My dad in return for that favor has had me removed from 2 spots and with the help of the rcmp put [me] on the street. I last checked. He recently bought a boat, a truck and an rv. Bought 4 weeks ago he invited me to stay in this rv. This is after I have struggled with finding a place for months. His new wife and him decided for whatever reason to have me removed from it without a face to face. Rcmp again. Now I have mention I am now on another 18 months probation because he had me charged with uttering threats. Which is bullshit. He again over the last couple years uses the incompetents and ingnorents of the rcmp since they like the idea of putting me in jail more then doing a better job of understanding the situation. My dad loves this fact and has found a decent way to rip off someone and use the rcmp as his strong arm. I have posted this in attempts to clear the air as to why I struggle recently. And to respond to a couple hurtful articles that were done. I didn't feel that was fair by my father since he did behind my back. Especially since his motives for doing so were not to help me as you can clearly read. Thanks to those who didn't turn their back on me. I will be fine. [*sic*]

It appears as though Stephen's relationship with Walter might be unsalvageable. It's a sad end for the young boy who longed and strived for his dad's attention. The boy who sweated and bled and fought for his father's love. The boy who sacrificed it all on the ice and showed his dad that he could make money playing hockey, just like the big guys on TV.

But despite massive challenges, and possibly years of mental health and addictions therapy ahead, there's still hope for Stephen Peat to get the help he needs and, possibly, to become healthy again.

CHAPTER 9

IT'S ALWAYS BEEN PART OF THE GAME

The fans are now getting involved ... as O'Reilly is out into the stands.
And this is going to be something. O'Reilly is into the stands, fighting
with a Ranger fan and all the Bruins are going over ... they're all into
the stands ... McNab's going up to grab somebody about seven or eight
rows up ...

Well, this is too bad that after the game is over it gets out of hand like
this ...

The Bruins are at a decided disadvantage, Fred, with those skates and
somebody could get seriously hurt.

This does the game no good at all ... and all the Bruins, it seems are
over the dasher and into the stands ... just a wild scene at Madison
Square Garden.

—Boston Bruins vs. New York Ranger fans
(Boston Bruins vs. New York Rangers, December 23, 1979)

FIGHTING HAS always been part of the game.

That right there is the most common argument I hear not only
for keeping fighting in the game but for celebrating the role it plays.
When all else fails, this is the argument that will be slapped down on
the table like a bible before a heretic. This line of argument is meant to
be unimpeachable in its wisdom and total in its finality. This argument
says: There's fighting in hockey, and that's just the way it is. End of story.

The argument has always made me laugh. Not only is it an appeal
to tradition, which is one of the most cringeworthy fallacies in the
world of debate, but from my perspective, it's also inherently untrue.
The actual game of hockey—the skating, the passing, the shooting—it
all stops when a fight takes place. The combatants square off to duke it
out, the referee blows the whistle, and everyone else stands and watches.

None of the fundamental activities of the game of hockey are taking place when bare fists are flying on the ice.

To be clear, I'm aware that's not exactly what fighting fans mean. They mean fighting is woven into hockey's DNA like a dominant gene. That fighting is not "other." That it's no different from the aforementioned skating, passing, and shooting. The argument is that fighting is simply a line item on that list, just as much a part of the game as the basics learned by children on rinks and ponds across the continent.

I do have to make at least one concession, though. If what fighting supporters are trying to say is that violence and roughness go back to the earliest known incarnations of the game, it turns out, they do have a point. Because in the very first recorded game of hockey, there was a fight.

Kind of.

On March 3, 1875, current and former students of McGill University (many of them also rugby players) took to the ice at the Victoria Skating Rink in Montreal, Quebec. And while it was the first recorded game of hockey, it was certainly not the first ever played.

Hockey has its roots in an English sport called bandy (played on skates on a football-sized ice surface where the players use bowed sticks and a ball), as well as shinty and Irish hurling (forms of field hockey originating on the British Isles with many similarities to one another). Hockey also draws inspiration from lacrosse and, of course, ice skating.

An article published in that day's edition of the *Montreal Gazette*[10] set the stage for an exciting sporting spectacle:

> A game of Hockey will be played at the Victoria Skating Rink this evening between two nines chosen from among the members. Some good fun may be expected, as some of the players are reputed to be exceedingly expert at the game.

Some fears have been expressed on the part of intending spectators that accidents were likely to occur through the ball flying about in too lively manner, to the imminent danger of lookers on. But we understand that the game will be played with a flat circular piece of wood, thus preventing all danger of its leaving the surface of the ice.

A couple of things here. They were playing with nine players a side! And they decided to use a wooden puck instead of a ball (like in bandy, shinty, hurling, and lacrosse), to allay the fears of the fans who didn't have boards or glass to protect them from the on-ice action.

From all accounts, the game was a big success. There was plenty of excellent end-to-end action and competition between sides. But it's what happened after the game that makes this story worth telling.

Near the end of the night, there was a violent confrontation. But it might not be exactly what you're expecting. Remember, this was basically the modern version of an intramural game between some McGill students. The fight didn't break out between the two teams but instead between the players and public ice skaters who were waiting to use the rink.

In the next day's edition of the *Montreal Evening Star*, there was an accusation from one of the public skaters, in the form of what must've been, based on the quick turnaround, a hastily written letter to the editor.[11]

The Victoria Rink

A Subscriber says: On going to the Victoria Skating Rink, last evening, at half-past seven, I was greatly surprised on being informed that it was to be monopolized by a select party in a game of shinny; the said parties did not make their appearance until a quarter-past eight, which tried the patience of all present. After this had commenced those not engaged waited with patience and pleasure until three games had been played which, in all sincerity, was considered by those not engaged in the tournament as a sufficient test of skill. By this time it was a quarter-past nine, they having thereby monopolized the Rink for one hour and three-quarters. A great number of subscribers, who had been there since the opening of the rink, considered they were entitled to a little amusement before leaving, and went on the ice for that purpose. The aforesaid select party thinking that possession was good law, attempted to drive the majority off, but finding they could not succeed in such a praiseworthy action, one of their number, in a most valiant manner assaulted some juveniles with his shinny stick … the players should not have resorted to personal violence, but have called upon the Rink guardians to clear the ice of the intruders.

Whoa, that's a serious allegation. The subscriber to the newspaper says the players assaulted some of the ice skating youths with their sticks! It seems as though a melee broke out, with intense argument to follow. All of this resulted in the ejection of many in attendance, our letter writer included.

This was all because, as the writer lays out, the public ice skaters were not aware that hockey had been scheduled to take over the rink that night, and those feelings of surprise and frustration were then exacerbated by the McGill players not taking to the ice until more than an hour after the paper advertised. The public skaters were pissed off, concluding that the hockey game had gone on long enough (a "sufficient test of skill"). With all of that anger, and the intrinsic Canadian need to skate, boiling to the surface, the skaters stormed the ice to get some laps in.

A very short article published in Kingston, Ontario's *Daily British Whig* two days after the game painted an even more alarming, and dangerous, picture.

The story read, in full: "A disgraceful sight took place at Montreal in the Victoria Skating Rink over a game of hockey. Shins and heads were battered, benches smashed and the lady spectators fled in confusion."[12]

This version makes it sound like the confrontation got pretty bad, with limbs and noggins taking the brunt of the damage.

So the very first game of hockey in recorded history involved violence, though not exactly the kind of hand-to-hand, bare-knuckle boxing I've been talking about in this book. In fact, most of the extreme early violence to emerge from the sport came in the form of stick swinging, rather than punching. Experts say there were brawls where punches were thrown, but not in the way we understand fighting in the modern context.

Professor Michel Vigneault, a hockey historian who wrote his Laval University dissertation on the early history of hockey, from 1875 to 1917, says that violence was relatively rare in the earliest years. From his perspective, the idea of fighting always being in the game is simply untrue.

"It's a big myth," he stated emphatically. "There [were] some fights in early hockey but not all the time. When you hear that fighting is part of hockey, it's not true. Because if you read all the accounts from the first ten to fifteen years of hockey, there's not very much fighting, if there's none at all. Fighting came later."

But not everyone agrees with Vigneault's assessment of fighting's infrequency in late-nineteenth-century hockey. Taylor McKee is a hockey scholar who studies media reaction to violence in the sport in the late nineteenth and early twentieth centuries. He says that although he began his research trying to debunk what he thought was the myth of commonplace violence in those early days of hockey, he quickly found out that his hypothesis was wrong.

"We can no longer argue that [violence] wasn't there," McKee declared. "It definitely was. But we also cannot argue that, essentially, people were fine with that. They were not. I know there's been resistance to violence in some fashion as early as the nineteenth century."

McKee points to an 1886 opinion article in the *Montreal Gazette* that harshly criticizes the perceived violence in a game between the Montreal Crystals and McGill University of the Amateur Hockey Association of Canada: "Every [hockey] game can be played without a trace of roughing and when this element comes into it, it becomes a sport no longer. The *Gazette* has before now waged war against the brutal part of some sports, and if hockey is to be played as it was last Friday, it has to be modified in some way."[13] According to this article, the roughness was so extreme that whatever was being played out on the ice definitely wasn't hockey—it wasn't even a sport at all!

McKee says this article, and others like it, contradict the assumption that violence has always been welcomed in the sport. "It's hard to argue that violence has always been an accepted part of the game," McKee said. "If eleven years in, and by a major publication, in the cradle of hockey civilization, they're saying, 'If it gets too rough, it's no longer a sport.'"

But despite the historians' takes on the role and prevalence of violence in hockey in those early years, there's no denying that it was most certainly influential. Hockey historian Kevin Slater (who is also on the board of the Society for International Hockey

Research) is an expert on the Ontario Hockey Association (OHA), an amateur league formed in 1891. He says the very genesis of that early league was prompted by a distaste for a certain level of violence that pervaded the game.

In 1890, an Ottawa team called the Rideau Rebels had just finished a short tour through southern Ontario that included the first ever game played in Toronto. During that Toronto game, there was violence, and it came as quite a shock to the Rebels players, who were well-to-do members of the capital city's social elite. Among the gentry were none other than two of Lord Stanley's sons (he of the Stanley Cup). We're talking about true-blue hockey royalty here.

"The Rebels were sort of dismayed at the barbaric ways hockey was being played," Slater said. "Not very organized, everybody having their own set of rules, the roughness that they encountered ... so they formed the OHA as a way of organizing all these different hockey clubs around Ontario and putting in place one set of rules for everybody to follow."

But even if the highfalutin Rideau Rebels didn't like the violence in hockey, there was one group of people that realized a few things: that roughness and aggression created tension, that tension created drama, and that drama sold, and sold well. We're talking about the newspapermen.

The reporting on games was a lot different back then. Whereas now, you get a brief synopsis of the game's starring players, the goals scored, some tactical developments, and other key moments (not to mention video highlights), back then, the write-ups read much more like lurid pulp fiction.

"There was a lot of exaggeration in how the game was reported seemingly, making it more exciting than it actually was," said Slater. "These people were trying to sell newspapers by writing exciting stories. So if you read game reports of the same game in multiple newspapers, the stories didn't always jibe. They didn't always sound like the same game even. It's a bit more fanciful writing than you would see in a report of the game now ... and the way it was written, every game was the most exciting game that was played in the rink this season."

And because the OHA's schedule featured mostly home-and-home series (back-to-back games against the same team, one in your rink, one in theirs) the newspapers only exacerbated the rivalries that came naturally with playing two games in a row. But, once again, it was more about "rough stuff," wrestling, melees, and even stickwork, than it was about toe-to-toe fighting as we know it in the modern sense.

"If the one team felt that they had been roughly used in the first game by the home team, that would sort of make it into the newspapers," Slater said. "And [they'd] say, 'We're not going to let that happen on our own rink when they come here next week,' which would sort of generate excitement around the game and those sorts of things would draw more fans because 'Wow, this is going to be a really hard-fought match, we gotta get even with these guys from the other town.'"

In these situations, the newspapers served as go-betweens for managers, players, and fans of the two teams, who would exchange what you might call some of the earliest forms of hockey trash talk.

"There would often be a back-and-forth in the editorials, [saying] 'The reporter from this newspaper says that we did this, but nothing could be further from the truth,'" Slater said. "And they would give their side of the story, and that would generate a lot of interest in the game. So it was all part of the hype and the generating of fan interest that was going into all this as well. The games might not have been as rough as it was made out to be in the newspapers. That may just have been the newspaper selling newspapers."

And in the early days of Ontario hockey, rough play found its way to the centre of a significant debate that would change the way the sport would evolve.

As hockey continued to grow in popularity, and it became more clear that it would be a money-making endeavour, professional leagues began to take over. The leaders of the amateur OHA were feeling the heat from the onslaught of the professionalization of the sport, and they didn't like it. So, what was the plan to preserve their little piece of amateur hockey heaven? They'd mount an offensive against the pro game, saying that it was played by single-minded hooligans hell-bent on aggression and assaults.

"The OHA was suggesting that the professional brand of hockey was rougher," Kevin Slater said. "That once you pay people to play hockey, they'll do anything to win, including smacking each other over the head with sticks and fighting, which you wouldn't see in the much more 'pure' OHA amateur version of the game."

Slater said that negative branding effort, along with being untrue and ineffective, was transparent. "It was obviously nonsense," he stated bluntly. "There were just as many fights in the OHA games as there ever were in the professional games."

Nevertheless, the amateur purists were right to be suspicious of the pro game because professionalism ended up sweeping across the hockey landscape and taking over the sport. And, yes, the violence continued. Although we don't have an exact date, or even year, for when glove-and-stick-dropping fights became the normalized pugilistic approach for pro hockey players, we do know that by the 1920s, bare-knuckle fighting was entrenched in the NHL.

Len Gould is a hockey historian who specializes in historical moving images of professional hockey. Len's main focus is on the violent side of the game. He says early NHL fist fights were not staged but fuelled by a range of emotions that topped out at "all-out rage."

"The scraps were separated by levels of emotion," Gould told me on the phone from his office in Florida. "You'll see some fights and you'll say, 'That's a fight.' These guys are pushing and shoving and slapping at each other, and it's nothing. And then you will see footage, and I'm telling you, it's like people literally trying to seriously injure one another. Like permanently hurt one another. So there's this real dichotomy."

Gould sent me copies of a couple of scraps from his archives. He wanted me to see just how vicious some of those old fights could be.

The first clip was the Montreal Canadiens playing the New York Rangers on March 17, 1935. After highlights of some of the rougher plays of the game (a couple big bodychecks and a dirty knee-on-knee hit), the video depicts a brutal explosion of violence when Nels Crutchfield, a centreman for the Montreal Canadiens, two-hands talented Rangers forward Bill Cook over the head with his stick. Cook begins to fall, but before he can hit the ice, Crutchfield appears to grab his head and slam him into the ground. A number of Rangers take exception, including Cook's brother Bun, and an all-out bench-clearing brawl ensues. There is no element of the "grab a partner and hang on" ethos that sometimes happens in modern NHL dust-ups. The punches being thrown are vicious haymakers, clearly intended to injure.

The next clip was truly difficult to watch. It was from the 1965 Memorial Cup Final between the Niagara Falls Flyers and the Edmonton Oil Kings. In the most grotesquely violent moment I've ever seen in hockey, Niagara Falls' Derek Sanderson (eventually of the

Boston Bruins) is standing beside Oil Kings captain Bob Falkenberg during a stoppage. Out of absolutely nowhere, Sanderson cocks back his fist as far as he can and lands the cheapest, most despicable sucker punch, possibly of all time. Falkenberg, who had previously received a five-minute major for spearing, is knocked out cold and falls to the ice. But somehow, Sanderson's not done. He pounces on his unconscious opponent like a mixed martial arts fighter and delivers six more vicious jackhammer punches. Falkenberg's head has the disturbing give of a leather throw cushion as the blows pound his face. He is taken from the ice on a stretcher.

That was the most brutal of the many instances of violence that took place during that '65 Memorial Cup. There were so many scraps, that were so one-sided, that pools of blood were visible on the ice, even in the black-and-white format. And as the game spiralled out of control, more than a dozen police officers swarmed the ice to calm the chaos.

So, extreme violence in hockey is not a new phenomenon, though you might argue that the violence from the old days was a bit more unabashed. Gould said this kind of behaviour is what led to the modern understanding of fighting as on-ice policing. The idea that the very possibility of a big tough dude coming out and fighting you would lead to safer behaviour from all players in the game.

"It's crap like this that birthed a culture where 'squaring up' and fighting was seen as the alternative to these maimings," Gould wrote in a later correspondence.

There were plenty of fights and even all-out bench-clearing brawls through the 1920s, '30s, '40s, and '50s, but as Gould told it, the story of fighting in hockey was changed forever by a young player from Vancouver, BC, who debuted for the Montreal Canadiens in 1963.

John Ferguson was called up to the Habs because he knew how to fight. But that's not to say he couldn't play a bit, too. Ferguson scored 145 goals in 500 career games and won five Stanley Cup rings. But the main reason Montreal wanted him was that he was tough, and could throw hands to protect his legendary line mate Jean Béliveau. Ferguson fought twelve seconds into his NHL debut, laying a beating on well-known agitator Ted Green of the Boston Bruins.

"I think [Ferguson] started lots of people at lots of different levels of hockey thinking about how this tool that's been in the tool box forever could be used in a different way," Gould said. And one of the guys who was inspired to think about that fighting tool in a different way was Fred Shero, the head coach of the Philadelphia Flyers, who led his infamous Broad Street Bullies team to consecutive Stanley Cup victories in 1973–74 and 1974–75. Although Shero swore he never explicitly told a player to fight, he is widely credited with being the first hockey mind to use on-ice fighting as a tactic of intimidation.

"Shero proved it could work, and he made it a tactic," Gould told me. "People realized John Ferguson, he was the Lamborghini of enforcers, but everyone else realized that you don't need a Lamborghini. You can sell plenty of Chevys and have more cars and more firepower. So all of a sudden you got this whole generation of guys who showed up where that's what they were there to do. That was the specialty."

Gould's Chevy metaphor is apt. The Flyers stats from those Cup years back it up. In 1973–74, the roster boasted no fewer than seven players with more than 100 penalty minutes. Notorious tough guy Dave Schultz had 348 PIMs all to himself. The next season, there were six players above 100 PIMs, with Schultz clocking in at an incredible 472 (that's an average of six minutes in the box every game!). That staggering number is still an NHL record, and the second-highest single-season total of all-time is a full 63 minutes behind.

The modern evolution of fighting through the 1980s, '90s, and 2000s is well documented, with most teams rostering multiple full-time enforcers whose main job was not to shoot and skate and score but to drop the gloves and fight on a near nightly basis. Those fighters, namely Bob Probert, Tie Domi, Gino Odjick, Stu Grimson, Tony Twist, Georges Laraque, Donald Brashear, Daniel Carcillo, and many, many more, were branded and marketed by their teams, the NHL, and hockey at large not as hockey players but as on-ice combatants.

Just like the newspapermen of the late nineteenth century, modern media has sold violence in hockey as not only an explosive on-ice sideshow but also a necessary part of the game and an essential viewing experience. And it's that normalization and celebration of bare-knuckle boxing on ice, throughout professional hockey history but particularly since the 1970s, that led to the stories in this book.

If not for that normalization, celebration, and cultural entrenchment of violence in hockey, James McEwan may never have felt compelled to fight to make his first junior roster. Stephen Peat may have focused more on skating, stick-handling, and defensive positioning than pulverizing his opponents. The same goes for Rick Rypien, Wade Belak, Derek Boogaard, and their enforcer contemporaries. All of their brains would be a lot better off for it too.

Now there's a new pro-fighting argument that's picking up steam and influencing the discussion. And this latest assertion is actually somewhat opposite to the traditional maxim we've been exploring in this chapter so far.

It goes like this: fighting numbers are way down. Or, if you want to frame it like the "always been part of the game" argument, you might say, "Fighting is barely even part of the game anymore."

And as it turns out, when it comes to the numbers, this argument is accurate. In the NHL, fighting is down sixty-nine percent over the past ten years (the decrease is almost the exact same over twenty years).[14] The 2018–19 season had the fewest fights in modern NHL history, with 226.

And if you look back further, the decrease is even more significant. In 1987–88, there were 925 fights, meaning there was an average of more than one fight per game played in the NHL that season. There has been an eighty-four-percent decrease in fighting since that time.

But the fact remains that if you watch an NHL hockey game, there is about a one in five chance that you'll witness a fight. So in 2018–19, there were still 226 bare-knuckle fights. That's 226 instances when gloves were dropped and blows were traded. Where young men received concussive and sub-concussive trauma to their brains.

The NHL has been notoriously reticent to discuss the impacts of concussions on its players. And questions about fighting are often met with guarded talking points about the practice being on its way out, despite the fact that it still happens regularly. In front of the cameras and microphones, NHL brass are extremely careful when they talk about fighting, but just a couple of years back, we got an inside peek at what the league's most powerful leaders think about the subject.

It was a case of NHL emails, first reported by TSN's Rick Westhead in March 2016. These messages are the closest you'll get to honest thoughts about fighting from head office. The emails were unsealed by a US federal court judge in Minneapolis, Minnesota, who was overseeing a class-action lawsuit against the NHL by former players seeking compensation for injuries brought on by traumatic brain injuries suffered on the ice. They were arguing that the league was putting profit before the health of its players.

The email chain was from September 2011, just after the consecutive deaths of Rypien, Belak, and Boogaard. Former all-star and then NHL chief disciplinarian Brendan Shanahan sent a *Globe and Mail* article entitled "Getting Rid of Hockey's Goons" by Eric Duhatschek to long-time NHL commissioner Gary Bettman and NHL executive vice-president and chief legal officer Bill Daly.

Bettman responded, "Do you remember what happened when we tried to eliminate the staged fights? The 'fighters' objected and so did the pa [NHLPA]. Eliminating fighting would mean eliminating the jobs of the 'fighters,' meaning that these guys would not have NHL careers. An interesting question is whether being an NHL fighter does this to you (I don't believe so) or whether a certain type of person (who wouldn't otherwise be skilled enough to be an NHL player) gravitates to this job (I believe more likely)."

Bill Daly raised the spectre of fighting leading to mental health issues and sometimes death. "I tend to think it's a little bit of both," Daly wrote. "Fighting raises the incidence of head injuries/concussions, which raises the incidence of depression onset, which raises the incidence of personal tragedies."

Bettman opined: "I believe the fighting and possible concussions could aggravate a condition. But if you think about the tragedies there were probably certain predispositions. Again, though, the bigger issue is whether the [NHLPA] would consent to in effect eliminate a certain type of 'role' and player."

Shanahan, the one who had started the email thread, and the only one with on-ice experience, weighed in about eliminating fighting: "The previous regime at the [NHLPA] definitely would fight it. But I thought their current position on illegal checks to the head is that it should encompass ALL contact. If we keep this simply about concussions and brain injuries then how can they argue against it."

Next, Shanahan admitted that hockey fighting had undergone wholesale changes since his playing days and disclosed to Bettman and Daly that drugs and alcohol were a common way of dealing with the fallout of fighting. "This is not the same role as it was in the '80s and '90s," he wrote. "Fighters used to aspire to become regular players. Train and practice to move from 4th line to 3rd. Now they train and practice becoming more fearsome fighters. They used to take alcohol or cocaine to cope ... Now they take pills. Pills to sleep. Pills to wake up. Pills to ease the pain. Pills to amp up ..."

Pills, pills, and more pills. These emails are proof that some of the most powerful people in the hockey world are aware of the reality of the lives of hockey enforcers. And this email exchange was from back in 2011. Yet still, all these years later, players like James McEwan, Stephen Peat, and others are living with the devastating consequences of bare-knuckle boxing on ice.

And in a much more recent example of a public airing of the NHL's attitude toward concussions and fighting, Commissioner Bettman travelled to Ottawa to testify before a group of Canadian politicians.[15] On May 1, 2019, he appeared before the House of Commons Subcommittee on Sports-Related Concussions. While his opening testimony outlined the NHL's concussion protocols, baseline medical testing, education programs, player assistance programs, and more, as you might expect, it also touched on fighting.

"Fights in the modern game are at an all-time low. Eighty-five per cent of regular season games are fight free which is the highest percentage of fight free games since the 1964–65 season," Bettman said. "With respect to concerns about fighting and concussions specifically, it is worth noting that relatively few concussions result from fighting. For example, based on video analysis of our games there have been an average of 2.6 diagnosed concussions per season over the last five seasons."

The most stunning moment of the seventy-five-minute hearing was when the commissioner was asked about the link between repeated traumatic brain injuries and CTE.

Nova Scotia Liberal Member of Parliament Darren Fisher asked a simple question: "What is your belief now and what is the league's position, these days, on whether there's a link between CTE and concussions?"

And what was Bettman's approach in the face of an ever-growing body of scientific evidence, not to mention an incredibly straightforward question? Deny, deny, deny.

"I'm not sure that the premise that the link is clear now is one that the scientific and medical community has embraced," he testified. "I am not a physician, I am not a scientist, my views are informed by experts in the field ... In short, I don't believe there has been, based on everything I've been told and if anybody has information to the contrary, we'd be happy to hear it, other than some anecdotal evidence, there has not been that conclusive link."

Chapter 5 of this book, which briefly summarizes the current scientific understanding of traumatic brain injuries and CTE, demonstrates that what Gary Bettman said was untrue. And that would not be the only time he was caught misleading the subcommittee.

At another point during his testimony, Bettman brought up a 2012 meeting he had with world leading CTE expert Dr Ann McKee, professor of neurology and pathology at Boston University's School of Medicine and director of BU's CTE Center. I cited her groundbreaking CTE diagnostic research earlier in the book.

"Dr Ann McKee ... told me in my office that hockey and football are not the same," Bettman told the MPs. "We don't have the repetitive head contact and impact that some of the other sports do, and so while we understand that this is an issue that needs to be constantly followed and focused on, there have not been conclusive determinations."

Only one day later, Dr McKee responded with a statement on Twitter.

"Mr Bettman misrepresented our 2012 conversation," she wrote. "Our research at Boston University and the VA-BU-CLF Brain Bank clearly shows that chronic traumatic encephalopathy (CTE) is associated with ice hockey play. We have found CTE in every former NHL player we have examined and we have also found it in amateur hockey players, some of whom had no significant fighting exposure. We would be delighted to have Mr Bettman visit the Brain Bank and discuss our research on CTE and repetitive brain trauma so that any future statements will more accurately reflect the state of the science."

And as it turned out, Dr McKee wasn't the only medical professional Bettman had to contend with in the fallout from his testimony. During MP questions, Dr Doug Eyolfson, a Manitoba Liberal Party MP and twenty-year ER doctor, pressed Bettman on why fighting is allowed in his league at all.

"You say we're at an all-time low for fighting and that it's 85% fight free," Dr Eyolfson began. "I would say that 15% have fighting and that's 15% too much. This is an act that is a criminal act in any other setting with perhaps the exception of the fighting sports like boxing. This could be removed from NHL hockey with the stroke of a pen ... The NHL could make rules that completely remove fighting from hockey. Completely. So why don't you?"

This assertion led to a feisty exchange between the commissioner and the MP. Bettman argued that he could not make changes to the rules without consulting with the NHLPA.

"It's interesting to say, we tolerate it, but it's a penalty," Bettman responded. "The answer is, it is penalized and the question you would have to ask is 'What would be the consequence of that act?'"

Bettman then turned to the tried-and-tested argument that claims fighting, and the threat thereof, actually makes the game safer and reduces brain injuries.

"The threat of other types of contact without the threat of fighting, as people who believe it's an important thermostat in the game is, would you rather see in an emotional moment a cross-check to the head, or an elbow to the head or a hit from behind?" Bettman asked. "The threat of fighting makes it clear that a level of conduct that is expected should be complied with."

When asked, Bettman was unable to cite any empirical evidence that fighting makes the game safer.

Oh, and even though Bettman was keen to point out that incidents of fighting in the NHL are decreasing, I can assure you that there's still plenty of fighting in the league. And it can still get really ugly, too.

Alexander Ovechkin is one of the greatest players to ever lace up skates. He is a Stanley Cup champion, a three-time MVP, a ten-time all-star, a Conn Smythe Trophy winner, a three-time World Champion, and a World Junior Champion. Ovechkin has led the NHL in goals eight times and sits thirteenth on the list of greatest goal scorers in league history. He will almost certainly finish his career among the top five goal-scorers of all time and go on to become a first ballot Hall of Famer.

But, for the 2018–19 season, Ovechkin won't be remembered for highlight reel goals, or for record-breaking performances. Instead, he'll be remembered for his role in one of the most devastatingly one-sided fights in recent memory.

The Washington Capitals, defending Stanley Cup champions, were taking on the Carolina Hurricanes in Game 3 of the first round of the NHL playoffs. That's when Ovechkin, not a fighter but still a hulking six-three, 236-pound thirty-three-year-old, hunted down and dropped the gloves with nineteen-year-old Andrei Svechnikov. At six-two and 195 pounds, the rookie was giving up more than forty pounds to his world-famous opponent. This really was a man fighting a boy with bare fists. And I'm sure you can guess what happened next.

Ovechkin landed a flurry of straight right hands to Svechnikov's face. The teenager crumbled to the ice. He was knocked out cold.

Pierre McGuire had the call for NBC: "Ovechkin and Svechnikov behind the play are getting after one another. Svechnikov's ready to fight with him ... HERE WE GO," McGuire bellowed.

But as it became clear that Svechnikov was unconscious, and badly injured, the broadcaster's tone shifted from excitement to one of desperation. "The kid's knocked out! You gotta get help! Get the trainer out there! Get out there! That's fighting out of your weight class. That's a KO. You admire the courage, but man oh man." Even Ovechkin appeared to gesture for the trainers after he delivered the damaging blow.

The game continued and Ovechkin returned to the ice after serving only five minutes in the penalty box. It was as though nothing had happened. Svechnikov most definitely did not return. He would miss more than two weeks recovering from a concussion.

I turned off the TV.

Now, what about the legal aspect of bare-knuckle boxing on ice?

Imagine you're walking down the street in downtown Toronto on a Friday night and two men start fist fighting on the street corner ahead. What do you do?

Well, you probably start by slowing down and keeping your distance. And then, if it's a serious punch-up, maybe you call the police.

The cops would be there in a hurry, and if the fighters were still around, they'd be immediately arrested and taken into custody.

You'd probably feel alarmed and be on high alert for a few minutes after, with the adrenaline pumping through your system like the last jolts from a waning caffeine buzz.

And it all makes sense. This kind of violence is unusual and unacceptable. We don't allow bare-knuckle fist fighting in civilized society. Punish those two guys and let's get on with our Friday night!

So why is hockey so different? Outside of the rink, we know exactly how to deal with violent, physical altercations. We use the criminal code to arrest and punish those who break it. We feel ill at ease at the sight of fighting, and in return, we choose not to tolerate it.

But in the world of hockey, it ain't so simple.

And let's be clear about another thing: bare-knuckle boxing, like the kind we see broadcast on the hockey highlights on a nightly basis, is illegal in Canada and in forty-seven American states. Only Mississippi, Florida, and Wyoming sanction bare-knuckle combat sports. That means bare-knuckle boxing is outlawed in the vast majority of North American society, except for in three states and tens of thousands of hockey rinks.

And the level to which hockey fighting is unregulated goes even further. The provincial and federal governments say they have nothing to do with regulating violence that takes place on the ice.

So hockey fighting is governed only by the hockey leagues themselves.

To be a bit more specific, the legal rules that allow for fighting in hockey go back to a 1991 Supreme Court of Canada decision called *Jobidon v. the Crown*.[16]

Back in 1986, Jules Jobidon fought Rodney Haggart outside a bar in Sudbury, Ontario. Jobidon knocked Haggart out with his first punch, and then continued to hit him. Haggart later died in hospital because of severe contusions to the head. Jobidon was charged with manslaughter, but he was acquitted at trial because he argued that Haggart had consented to the fight. That verdict was overturned in the Court of Appeal for Ontario, and Jobidon was convicted of manslaughter.

Five years after the initial fight and subsequent death of Rodney Haggart, the Supreme Court of Canada upheld the appeal court ruling of manslaughter for Jules Jobidon.

Basically, before this case, it was understood that if two people wanted to settle their differences outside a barroom or on the street, that was acceptable. But the *Jobidon* ruling changed that line of thinking, saying one cannot consent to being assaulted and suffering "serious hurt or non-trivial bodily harm."

Now, you might be wondering why hockey players are allowed to consent to these kinds of fights on the ice. It's because the Supreme Court justices thought specifically about sports like hockey in their decision. The *Jobidon* ruling made explicit exceptions for fighting and rough play in sports, as long as they fall within the customary norms of the game. Here's that key part of the ruling from the conclusion, written by Justice Charles Gonthier on behalf of the five–two majority:

> The policy of the common law will not affect the validity or effectiveness of freely given consent to participate in rough sporting activities, so long as the intentional applications of force to which one consents are within the customary norms and rules of the game. Unlike fist fights, sporting activities and games usually have a significant social value; they are worthwhile ...
>
> The court's majority determined that some forms of intentionally applied force will clearly fall within the scope

of the rules of the game, and will therefore readily ground
a finding of implied consent, to which effect should be
given. On the other hand, very violent forms of force which
clearly extend beyond the ordinary norms of conduct will
not be recognized as legitimate conduct to which one can
validly consent.

This part of the ruling is crucial because it lays the legal groundwork
for allowing bare-knuckle boxing in hockey, specifically because of
the use of the term "customary norm."

Fighting is expressly not allowed in the rules of hockey. But
we're not talking about rules here; we're talking about customary
norms. One might argue the very fact that fighting is mentioned,
written down in black ink in the hockey rule book, indeed makes
it something that regularly happens in the game, something that is
to be expected. That is, a customary norm.

"It is an interesting artifact of our law that this 'customary norm'
concept exists," explained Vancouver criminal defence lawyer Eric
Gottardi. "And that's where this kind of implied permission for the
repeated assaults that we witness every night when we're watching
our local hockey games is accepted. There's this sense that within the
norm and the context of the hockey game there are infractions that
are prohibited by the rules and there are consequences for those."

Implied consent is an important term to understand as well.
Basically, it means that by putting on gear, lacing up skates, and
hitting the ice, hockey players are giving their consent to be assaulted
and injured within those aforementioned customary norms of the
game. The idea of implied consent might be clear to most adults who
play the game at a competitive level. But some people, like hockey
historian Taylor McKee, author of the scholarly article "A Separate

Reality: Contextualizing, Creating and Curating Definitions of Canadian Hockey Violence," wonder if it's fair to assume teenagers playing major junior and junior A have fully considered what that implied consent really means. McKee said, "The fact is that sixteen-year-olds could think to themselves, 'Man, I might have to do this.' Not, that it could happen, 'I might have to do it as a part of the necessary conditions of being a hockey player,' and that, in my humble opinion, is insane. That's something when you're twelve, thirteen, fourteen, fifteen years old, you're not capable of making these kinds of bargains."

McKee uses the notorious Steve Moore/Todd Bertuzzi incident as an example. Bertuzzi is famous for making one of the dirtiest plays of all time back in 2004. Steve Moore had delivered a couple of questionable bodychecks to Vancouver Canucks captain Markus Näslund that game and earlier in the season. Bertuzzi hit the ice looking for retribution. But when Moore opted not to drop the gloves and instead turned away, Bertuzzi dropped his right glove and sucker punched Moore in the side of the head. Moore was knocked out cold and lay on the ice unconscious for around ten minutes. He had three fractured vertebrae, facial cuts, and a serious concussion.

"If Steve Moore would have been killed there, they would have had a very, very difficult time putting [Bertuzzi] in jail," McKee opined. "Because you can't possibly say, because of the collective experiences of 100 years of organized hockey, that he couldn't have expected Todd Bertuzzi to do that."

At that point, McKee drew an unexpected comparison. "We've created this system of hockey where there's essentially an unlimited liability," McKee said. "When you're fourteen, do you know that? Do you realize that you're signing up for that kind of unlimited liability, the stuff we only really associate with signing up for war?

The idea that you could be killed on that ice surface and we can just say, 'Meh, that's just the game.' It's the only other situation I can think of where we allow young people in our country, our citizens, to sign away their abilities to say, 'I'm protected under the law.'"

And there's one last part of that *Jobidon* ruling that deserves some scrutiny. In a sweepingly general statement it says, "Unlike fist fights, sporting activities and games usually have a significant social value; they are worthwhile." I think most of us would agree that this statement is essentially true. But one could also argue that it's not nearly specific enough. It's basically saying that sports, as they are and as they have always been, are valuable, full stop. Therefore, what happens within the game, even if it's violent and dangerous, is acceptable. It strikes me that each sport has various aspects that are more valuable and less valuable than others. Based on the devastating stories I've outlined in this book, it seems clear that fighting in hockey is an aspect of the sport that is objectively less valuable.

And that brings us all the way back to that age-old idea that fighting has always been a part of the game of hockey. No matter how problematic that argument is, it has been incredibly influential. So influential, and so pervasive, in fact, that it is, in essence, the linchpin in the key Supreme Court ruling that ostensibly allows for bare-knuckle boxing on ice. Fighting in hockey is considered a customary norm, and the Supreme Court makes violent allowances for customary norms.

And that begs one of the most important questions of all: How is it that an archaic argument, with a questionable level of truth behind it, has become so entrenched in our broader culture that it informs the highest law of the land? The *Jobidon* Supreme Court ruling and its exceptions for sports makes it clear that, in Canada, it is not the law that dictates hockey culture. In fact, it is hockey culture, with all of its inherent violence, that dictates the law.

PART 3: DALE PURINTON

CHAPTER 10
BROTHERHOOD

We're gonna get a fight on the far side ... Purinton going at it ... He's
with Stephen Peat, the twenty-one-year-old. Stephen Peat, one of the
rookies, making the start in this, his second game ... Purinton and
Peat, it has a nice ring to it. Sounds like a law firm. You might need
one if they play that way all year.
—Dale Purinton vs. Stephen Peat
(New York Rangers vs. Washington Capitals, October 10, 2001)

THIS NEXT story got me thinking a lot about friends: how they meet
and how they grow together. So, for a bit of inspiration, I looked up
some songs about friendship. Dozens have been recorded and the most
famous are considered some of pop music's all-time greatest tunes.

Take, for example, James Taylor, who promised that you could
just call out his name and wherever he was, he'd come running.
Then there were the Rembrandts, who famously sang, "I'll be there
for you" during the opening credits of TV's legendary *Friends*. Jack
White sang about young kids having an adventure on their way
to school and looking for bugs and worms in "We're Going to Be
Friends." And, of course, according to the Beatles, you can always
get by (and high) with a little help from your friends.

Those are the feel-good tunes. But there are all kinds of friends,
even some who aren't always what they're cracked up to be. There
are Garth Brooks's friends in low places and friends getting into all
kinds of trouble in Chance the Rapper's "Summer Friends." And, of
course, Biz Markie wasn't buying it when his girl told him that the
other guy was just a friend.

During my shallow dive into friendship songs, I found a great
range of stories, ideas, and emotions. Lots of great hooks too! But

no matter how hard I tried, I couldn't find a soundtrack for the friendship between Stephen Peat and Dale Purinton. I guess repeatedly punching someone in the face with bare fists and then going on to befriend them has yet to be captured by the great songwriters. You might even venture to say that this kind of friendship isn't all that common. Not outside the hockey world, anyway.

Friends do sometimes meet under unusual circumstances, to be sure. But this is next level. When you think back to the strangest way you ever met one of your friends, I'm guessing your opening line probably wasn't "Wanna go?" To regular folk, it might seem crazy that a bare-knuckle boxing match in front of 20,000 fans would be a fertile breeding ground for a lasting friendship. But for Purinton and Peat, that's exactly what happened.

As with so many hockey players who earn their living on the fighting fringes, Dale and Stephen first met on the verge of combat. Peat was a tough, cocky sixteen-year-old taking the WHL by force for the Red Deer Rebels. Purinton was the proverbial heavyweight champion of the league with the Lethbridge Hurricanes.

"Peaty came into the Western League beating the shit out of everyone," Purinton remembered. "And he beat up all the twenty-year-olds, tough fuckers too, that I knew. So we played Peaty one night and Peaty's asking me to go and I said, 'Well, when you earn it, I'll fight ya,' but the truth is ... I didn't want to take a chance to lose."

So in the beginning, Peat was the young upstart trying to knock the king, Purinton, from his tough-guy throne. You can almost hear the immortal words from the end of *Casablanca*: "I think this is the beginning of a beautiful friendship." Am I right?

"Rocky Thompson and Wade Belak and all those guys were gone [from the WHL]. They all turned pro the year before me, so I was killing everyone and I had no one to fight really," Purinton added. "And I couldn't take the chance of losing against Peaty because he was a sixteen-year-old. And I wasn't sure [if I would win] 'cause he was killing it."

But despite Purinton's success keeping the gloves from hitting the ice during that first meeting in junior in 1996, he and Peat would cross paths again in the pros. In fact, their first scrap broke out less than four minutes into Stephen's second NHL game, directly in front of the New York Rangers' bench at Madison Square Garden. And their violent relationship would only blossom from there.

"I ended up fighting Peaty a couple of times," Purinton said. "And he was a super tough guy ... like, dangerous."

The enforcers exchanged nasty words, plenty of wrestling, and a couple of haymakers, but little did they know that they were also seeding a meaningful relationship that would later bloom at a time when both men would be facing daunting challenges in their personal lives.

The thing that's hard for the rest of us to understand is that hockey fighting is a brotherhood. The job is so singular, so punishing, and so far beyond the realm of regular work that it makes sense that these guys share a common gravitational force. They understand each other. They just get it. Purinton told me that he followed all of his fighting foes in the NHL closely, Stephen Peat included.

"There's so much to it, man," Dale said. "Once you're in the league for a bit, you know each other and you pull for [them]. If a young guy's doing well, we'd talk and it's kind of like you stick together. You get older and guys have mortgages and families, and you want them to keep their jobs. So there's so much more to it than just 'Oh, two guys are goin' out to fight.' You become united almost when you're in the league for a while."

The biggest bond of all, the one that transcends even the exchange of expertly thrown punches, is the shared knowledge of how hard they train, how hard they punch, and how hard it hurts. "You respect each other," Purinton told me. "You watch each other ... no one plays like us. It's the hardest job in that league."

And it's that indelible connection between fighters that made the tragic deaths of Wade Belak, Rick Rypien, and Derek Boogaard back in 2011 so difficult for fighters to absorb. Enforcers across the continent saw themselves in those men who died. Integrating the deaths into their lives and, by extension, gaining a deeper understanding of their own mortality, for many, was a tough pill to swallow. Dale Purinton counts himself among those who were devastated by the news. "They're like your brothers, right?" he said. "They're basically the same as you. They live the same lifestyle, they grew up the same, they have the same job. You just relate so much to them."

Purinton has proudly represented that brotherhood of the fighter and showed his friendship for Stephen Peat by reaching out to him when he landed in rehab on Vancouver Island. He wanted to see Peat bounce back from the brain injuries, the drugs, the homelessness, and the jail time. "It's heartbreaking knowing he's struggling," Purinton said. "I would do anything for him. It's terrible."

Dale wants the same for all of his fellow former enforcers. That's why he lobbied high-profile American politicians in Washington, DC, to take a closer look at concussions in pro hockey. That's why he was one of the leaders of a class-action lawsuit against the NHL.

But it turns out Dale, like so many fighters, has a harrowing story of his own. His journey has taken him through the depths of drug and alcohol abuse, estrangement from his family, and the prospect of hard time in a maximum-security American prison.

Picture a twenty-three-year-old Canadian hockey player hitting the ice at Madison Square Garden. He feels the cold wind on his face and the smooth ice under his skates. The spotlights track across the dark ice surface as 20,000 fans welcome him with a thunderous roar.

This is midtown Manhattan, New York City. The centre of the universe for sports, arts, and entertainment. And within New York City, MSG is the epicentre of the biggest, most important entertainment there is on the planet. The lights don't get any brighter. The fans don't get any crazier. The media doesn't get any fiercer. When the phrase "hitting the big time" was coined, this has to be what the originator had in mind.

But wait just a second. Let's hit that rewind button. Go back, back, back, nineteen years to 1981, and that same kid, four years old, is riding his bike in the middle of a quiet rural street in sleepy Sicamous in central British Columbia.

Now, you may not think bike riding is all that noteworthy for a four-year-old. Almost every kid does it. But that bike was the only one the Purinton family owned. It was the only bike for TEN kids. Dale Purinton was the youngest of his six brothers and three sisters.

"I'd be riding that bike, and I'd be the first one right on that bike," Dale reminisced. "And I'd be with some of my friends and I'd see my brother walking with his buddies and being like, 'Hey guys!' and being nice to us, and all they were doing was sucking me into knocking me off my bike. So this was like an ongoing thing with food and everything. You were just tough or not, right? You are tough or you put up with it."

Starting at the ripe young age of four, Dale was fighting for his bike, for his food, and for his place in the world. And it only progressed from there. Dale fought in school, he fought on the street, he fought in the bar, and eventually, he fought all the way to the National Hockey League.

This is the unlikely story of how Dale Purinton went from being knocked off his bike on a tiny hobby farm in a BC resort town, to Madison Square Garden, to the depths of drug and alcohol abuse, and all the way to a New York State maximum-security prison and back again.

Dale Purinton was born in Fort Wayne, Indiana, in the heart of basketball country, not exactly what you'd call a hockey town. His dad, Cal Purinton, played parts of nine seasons for the minor pro International Hockey League (IHL) Fort Wayne Komets (between 1963 and 1973). Cal was a rough-and-tumble defenseman, racking up 1,293 penalty minutes and thirty-two goals in 516 professional games. That's a lot of rough stuff. It would appear Dale came by his vocation honestly.

When I spoke with Dale on the phone, I asked him about his first hockey moments. Stepping onto the ice, scoring his first goal, maybe receiving hand-me-down gear from his siblings.

No can do. That's not possible, he told me, because hockey was such an all-encompassing, dominant force in his life, he doesn't remember a time when he didn't have a stick in his hands or skates on his feet. "I don't even remember not playing," he said. "I don't even think we had cable, but you could get *Hockey Night in Canada*. If we weren't at the rink, we'd be playing street hockey."

Dale does have one early memory that sticks out. And it sticks out hard. Dale was five years old and it was his first season playing at the brand-new rink in Sicamous. He saw a teammate doing snow angels after a game, so he did what any other kid would do: he laid down on the chopped-up, snowy ice to join in the fun. He was having an absolute blast, but his mother, not so much.

"She's over the glass yelling at me to get off the ice," Purinton said. "And I guess another mom's like, 'Look at them, they're so cute,' and my mom's pounding on the glass saying, 'Get up!'"

After Dale made his way off the ice, his mother, Dulayne, delivered a scorching speech that has stuck with him for the rest of his life.

"She said, 'Okay, I'm going to tell you something right now,'" Dale remembered, sounding one part serious, one part on the verge of belly laughter. "'Hockey is very expensive ... You're not playing hockey for fun. You're playing hockey to get something out of it, and to learn, and to work. If you want to have fun, I'll buy you a fucking colouring book and crayons.'"

Harsh words from a parent, to be sure, but Dale says it lit a lasting fire within him. "She was just ruthless. But honestly, without her there's no way I would have played," he said. "My parents dedicated their lives and pretty much gave up everything they had so they could support us all."

Whereas his mom brought the aggression, Dale's dad, the former pro player, was much more analytical and philosophical about the game. With Cal, it was all about instilling focus and work ethic.

"My dad did such a good job," Purinton said. "He would always say ... 'When you're at practice be first at every drill and first in the line. Be the hardest-working guy on the team.' Even if we lost, or even if I played bad, he would never say it. He wasn't a grinder. He just said, 'Work hard, man.' So he was awesome that way."

But even with the thoughtful feedback from his old man, Purinton sometimes felt as though the family's seriousness surrounding hockey sucked some of the joy out of it. "He kind of ruined hockey for me because I wasn't allowed to be a fan, I had to be a student," Purinton explained. "He would just get me to watch certain guys on TV and say, 'Hey, watch how this guy is playing, see how he moves the puck?' So he really taught me the IQ of the game early on."

But whether the game brought joy to his life or not, Dale excelled. He was big, strong, and tough. And he wasn't afraid to make life difficult, and often painful, for his opponents.

When I asked Dale to take me through his first ever hockey fight, he hesitated. He couldn't remember that first scrap. Purinton told me there were so many fights, in the yard, at school, and on the ice, that there wasn't really a memorable starting point. Fighting was just always there. Constant, like sunrise, sunset, breakfast, lunch, and dinner.

But there was one early fight that Dale remembered well. Maybe because it could've been the first hockey fight with serious conse- quences for the other guy. Purinton said he was fourteen years old, and the family had moved from Sicamous to Calgary, Alberta. He and his brother Chris (who was eighteen at the time) were playing summertime drop-in hockey on opposing teams in a meaningless game of shinny.

Meaningless, that is, until Dale's brother started a confrontation.

"So, my brother gets into it with a guy on my team whose, like, a man," Dale told me. "It started getting heated up, and finally, the guy sticks my brother and my brother sticks him back."

Brother-on-brother fisticuffs are no huge surprise in hockey. In fact, fights between Wayne and Keith Primeau, and Eric and Marc Staal have been celebrated as special moments in the annals of hockey-fighting history. So I was anticipating that Dale might have dropped the mitts with his big bro. That this was a story about brotherly love put on hold for a shinny dust-up. I anticipated wrong.

"I literally jumped the bench and drop the gloves and just pounded the shit out of this guy," Dale remembered. "He had, like, a big mustache. [After] we just left the rink, got changed, and left.

If you did that now, you'd probably have assault charges. But that was almost thirty years ago. So, that's sort of my first one."

As Purinton grew bigger and stronger, the hockey fights increased in frequency, and so did the decisions in his favour. He could change the game with his very physical presence, and he knew it. So, at the age of seventeen, and after just a couple of seasons in junior, Dale put his name forward for the NHL entry draft. The draft was held at the Northlands Coliseum in Edmonton, Alberta, only about 300 kilometres (186 miles) north of his family home in Calgary. His entire family was there in box seats, waiting for the big moment.

Dale was drafted by the New York Rangers (round 5, 117th overall) in the same draft class as hockey legends and future Hall of Famers Jarome Iginla and Shane Doan.

Purinton had achieved a lifelong goal. His path to the NHL was laid out in front of him. And what did Dale do to celebrate? He doubled down on the huge amount of work he was already putting in. More effort, more training, and more focus. Dale finished out his junior career with an eye on the big show.

Building on an already impressive pugilistic skill set, Dale's fighting ability reached a new level when he was traded from the Kelowna Rockets (where he played only twenty-two games) to the Lethbridge Hurricanes at the age of nineteen. Back in Alberta, he started working with a local trainer named Trevor Hardy of HARD Training. According to Dale, Hardy has trained some of hockey's toughest customers, including Bryce Salvador, Byron Ritchie, and Chris Phillips. Fighting was a big part of the training regimen, including a good dose of boxing and ground fighting, but it went beyond that too. This training was the most thorough, and relentless, that Purinton had ever experienced.

"Honestly, out of all the trainers I've ever trained with, all the hockey guys in all the NHL cities, [Trevor] was by far, to me, the primo guy," Purinton stated emphatically. "That was a turning point for me when I met him and we started going to work and training and training and training and training."

Looking back, Dale realized that he may not have actually made the NHL without that next-level training, but he also knows that particular training unlocked his ability to fight bigger, tougher, and more punishing opponents. With years of perspective on his side, Purinton wonders whether gaining that elite fighting ability was actually a good thing.

"That really put me in a category where I could really start messing with the real big heavyweights," Dale said. "Because I was strong enough, but I wasn't big enough in a way because I'm six-two, right? Other guys were six-five. But then I got so strong and powerful and could punch so hard that I could fight any of those guys, but at what cost?"

To be clear, Purinton's current trepidation about fighting exists only in hindsight. In real time, he was punishing his opponents with zeal. Dale relished the fights and the influence they had on the game. He was a hockey fighter. And he loved it.

After his twenty-year-old season in the WHL, Dale had a thirty-four-game stint with the Charlotte Checkers of the ECHL, and then was quickly promoted to the Hartford Wolf Pack of the AHL. He was so close to the big leagues he could taste it.

After an injury-shortened season with the Wolf Pack, where he played in forty-five games and spent 306 minutes in the penalty box, Purinton wrought hell on his opponents during the 1999–2000 season. He played sixty-two games and racked up a staggering 415 PIMs, with four goals and four assists to boot. At the end of the season, he was called up for one game with the big club. Dale was set to make his NHL debut in a rivalry matchup between the New York Rangers and the Philadelphia Flyers.

Dale logged a healthy twelve minutes and forty-five seconds of ice time, and in the third period, he saw his chance to do what he did best. He dropped the gloves with two-time all-star and Canadian Olympian Keith Primeau. At six-five and 220 pounds, Primeau was a big boy. Despite giving up three inches in height, getting trapped in a head lock early, and taking a few Primeau punches, Purinton acquitted himself well, giving just about as much as he got. We'll call it a draw.

Dale must've made a strong impression during that one-game tryout, because he ended up spending most of the next four years as a member of the New York Rangers. He played 181 NHL games in all. And this wasn't just any old NHL team. In the early 2000s, the Rangers were absolutely stacked with legendary talent. Dale played alongside hockey royalty like Mark Messier, Brian Leetch, Jaromír Jágr, Pavel Bure, Theoren Fleury, Eric Lindros, Petr Nedved, and Mike Richter. It was an insane collection of superstars and a dream come true. Such were the perks of playing for the fabled Original Six franchise. Purinton told me he became close with Messier, to the point that he and his wife were married at the captain's home in the Bahamas.

But as with most enforcer stories, the good times didn't last. An incident during a 2004 game against the New Jersey Devils changed the course of Dale's career, and his life. He suffered a serious concussion that came not from a fist but from a skate.

"I got kicked in a pile and a skate hit me right under the chin," Dale said. "It was the only time I've ever been knocked out, and I fell flat on my face. I think there was six games left and I missed them. After that, I don't think I was ever the same again."

CHAPTER 11

WE'RE SUPPOSED TO BE WARRIORS

Uh-oh ... Purinton and Brashear. You talked about having a party,
here's a party.
—Dale Purinton vs. Donald Brashear
(New York Rangers vs. Philadelphia Flyers, March 7, 2003)

DALE RE-SIGNED with the Rangers following the 2004 season. But because of the NHL lockout and the cancellation of the season, Purinton wouldn't be patrolling the wing at Madison Square Garden. Instead, he played for the Victoria Salmon Kings in the ECHL, two full steps below the national league.

But whether his season was played in the big leagues or on the farm, Dale's life was headed in the wrong direction. He was starting to feel the pressure of the nightly fights. He was filled with dread. He'd come to see the fighting as a vicious spectacle rather than a valuable part of the game.

Dale turned to drugs and alcohol to ease the pain. "I started really self-medicating because of pressure, and I really felt that we were just animals in a circus and people were coming to watch us," Purinton reflected. "I kind of quit training, and I just didn't want to do it anymore. I didn't have the fire I once had. And I just knew ... I knew something wasn't right. I just kept playing 'cause that's all I knew, right?"

At the age of twenty-seven, Dale was still relatively young and could lean on his strength and experience to survive the nightly scraps. But everything felt a bit off.

"When you don't have that fire to train six hours a day in the summers and put in an extra hour every day to be the best-shape guy, that's how guys get in trouble," he said. "And that's how guys eventually get hurt."

Although the consumption of drugs and alcohol seems to be an unofficial line on the hockey enforcer's job description, Dale hadn't done much drinking or drugs until his mental health started to suffer late in his career. "I got into self-medicating, having anxiety, bouts of depression, but I kind of kept it quiet," he said. "I started using lots of drugs, lots of alcohol, nights before games. I didn't really start partying until I turned pro."

Purinton's injury from that skate to the head was devastating. It affected him for months. Only the substances were providing temporary relief. But for Dale, the saddest part was that his love for the game had been tainted. All he had ever done was strive to be the best and honour the sport, but sustaining that love was becoming next to impossible. He was stuck in a cycle of drinks, drugs, and dread.

"I loved hockey, just wanted to be a hockey player," he said. "And as the pressure started building up, and I got hurt like that, I didn't even want to go to the rink anymore. The night before, I felt like I didn't want to do it, so I would just drink and take sleeping pills or what have you, whatever the night was like. I'd go to sleep, go play a game, and do it all over again."

Dale's reflexive physical aversion to playing was so intense that he took to vomiting before every game. "I would always dry heave and try to be throwing up because I've been so sick to my stomach before the game was about to start," Dale remembered. "Because I would always jump guys. I was dirty, right? So I had all these guys who were coming after me, big guys in the lineup. So I would just drink myself into oblivion, take Ambien, or do both, then I'd be kind of hungover for the game, so I'm not fuckin' feeling right anyway. And it just kept getting worse and worse."

Dale wasn't joking about being a dirty player. Between his AHL and NHL careers, he was suspended thirteen times for infractions like eye gouging, sucker punching, and kneeing. He was even suspended for seven games in 2001 for cross-checking his friend Stephen Peat in the head.

Dirty play aside, the combination of the dread and the substances meant Dale's hockey career was quickly coming to a close. After the lockout-cancelled season, he would never suit up for the Rangers again. Dale spent parts of three seasons in the AHL with the Wolf Pack, then the Lake Erie Monsters. He retired in 2008, at the age of thirty-one.

After his playing days were done and the on-ice brawls were a thing of the past, Dale's life improved. He and his wife, Temple Greenleaf, had three young sons and their family life was good, living in a small town called Shawnigan Lake on Vancouver Island. He quit drinking and doing drugs. The anxiety and depression visited less often. He still had mood swings, but they were controllable. Dale started coaching the junior A Cowichan Capitals of the BCHL. For about five years, it seemed like Dale might live a regular post-hockey life, raising kids and coaching the sport he loved.

But the good times came to a sudden and grinding halt in 2014, when Purinton's mother, Dulayne, died. He was devastated and had no idea how to cope. Purinton spiralled into the deepest depression he had experienced in years. The pain was immeasurable, and the only way he knew how to manage was with drugs and booze. But this time, he took his drug use to the next level, turning to opioid painkillers.

"Because I'd done drugs in the past, I wasn't afraid of it and I'd just do whatever, and it actually made me happy because I'd be depressed all the time," Dale said. "I was super sad, so then when I took those things I was like the happiest guy ever. I was like, 'Holy shit, this is a cure.' And obviously that shit gets out of control, right? And you got sick without it. It just fuckin' takes off on you."

Dale used drugs and drank heavily for months after his mother's death, and finally, after a lot of stress and many confrontations, his wife decided she wanted him out of the family home. "The police removed me from my house because my wife said I was dangerous," he said. "I was high all day ... I was out of the house for three months until I flew to New York."

Dale went back to New York because his wife was flying there to visit her parents with the kids in the summer of 2015. She had invited him to come to her family's cabin in Oneida County, and he was excited at the chance to patch things up and possibly start over.

But Dale's lifetime of using his fists to solve problems, combined with a big infusion of alcohol, once again got in the way. After a couple of quiet nights in with the kids, Dale and his wife went out with a bunch of family and friends to celebrate a birthday. Dale dove into the booze hard. Everything started off great. Dale was the life of the party, telling stories and buying rounds, but his inebriation made him susceptible to jealousy, especially since his relationship with his wife was so shaky at the time.

Later in the evening, after countless drinks, Dale's wife asked him to take a group photo with her phone. This might seem like an innocuous request, but it was actually the beginning of a terrible chain of events fuelled by Purinton's bad decisions.

While he was holding his wife's phone, a man from Temple's past texted her. Dale says the texts urged his wife to leave him and take up with the hometown guy instead. The man was telling Temple that he loved her now and always had.

In an unfortunate twist of fate, the guy texting Temple lived right across the street from the bar they were in. He was right there, and Dale knew it. Purinton went outside. The texter was standing out on his porch. Dale crossed the street and confronted him. What followed was brutally violent.

"I said, 'Are you texting my wife, you piece of shit?'" Dale remembered solemnly. "And he said, 'Oh, we're just friends,' and so I grabbed him and I go to push him against the door, but we smash through the door. So I beat the shit out of this guy really bad. I was drunk ... and fuck, it was bad. Like collapsed lung, broken ribs, he almost choked to death. He was in the ICU for a while. I didn't know for a couple of days if he was going to live."

Dale knew it was bad at the time, too. He left the scene and went back to the cabin where he and his family were staying. After a week-long investigation, police tracked him down and arrested him. Dale was expecting an assault charge, but instead, he was charged with burglary, the broken-down door used as the evidence. In New York, burglary is a Class B violent felony and carries with it a sentence of anywhere between five and twenty-five years. By comparison, a second-degree assault charge would have carried a maximum sentence of seven years. The severity of the charge meant it was likely Dale would be extradited from Canada to face charges in the United States. Even without a prior record, he faced the possibility of being separated from his kids for a big chunk, if not all, of their childhood. And who knows what it might've meant for his marriage, which was already hanging on by a thread.

With a trial looming but still months away, Purinton made bail and returned to Vancouver Island. He had a friend who owned the Cedars at Cobble Hill treatment centre in Victoria. He went straight there and checked in.

"Because they turned it into a felony, then I got arrested, [the story] went national," he said. "I could have killed the guy, [so] I have to be accountable and that's what got me sober. I got the treatment and that's what kind of changed my life."

Dale completed three months of treatment, and just a couple of weeks after he got out, his lawyers informed him he had a big decision to make. A plea deal was on the table. If he took it, he'd have to pay a significant sum to the victim and spend six months in a maximum-security prison on a misdemeanour assault charge. If he rejected the deal, he'd face trial, with the possibility of serving up to twenty-five years behind bars.

The risk of a trial was too much for Dale to fathom. He took the plea deal and made the familiar trip back to New York. But this time, he would not be competing in front of thousands of fans at Madison Square Garden. He would not be spending time with his family in cabin country. This time, he would face the consequences of his violent actions in a maximum-security unit at the Mohawk Correctional Facility in Oneida County.

At the time, Purinton's children were nine, seven, and six. What do you tell young kids when their dad goes away to jail for nearly half a year? He and his wife couldn't bring themselves to explain the painful situation they were facing, so they told the boys that Daddy had to go away for work.

"I actually got to Skype every day with them," Dale said. "And you get to wear a white T-shirt, so you don't have to wear a jumpsuit or anything. I said I was baking, which is true. I was in the kitchen, so I was baking pancakes and stuff for the whole prison, you know?"

Now that his kids are getting older, Dale's trying to figure out the best way to tell them the truth. The truth that their dad made a horrible mistake that endangered someone's life. The truth that their dad was suffering from addiction at the time. And the truth that even when life is at its bleakest, there is always something to be learned and self-improvement to be made.

"One day we'll sit down and tell them, you know, there are consequences," Purinton told me. "I wasn't well at the time that I made those choices. Some people see the wake-up calls, and some don't. And so for me, that was one where I had to get sober and never use again, and that was my last chance. Next time it could be death, or next time I could go to jail for life. It actually ended up being the biggest gift I ever received."

Dale had come face-to-face with his moment of reckoning, and despite some dire consequences—namely, serious injury to another person, months in a maximum-security prison, further estrangement from his wife and kids, and national headlines touting his transgressions—he had come out the other side sober and ready to do better. Better by his family and better by his fellow hockey enforcers.

When Dale returned to Vancouver Island from prison in New York, he was focused, firstly, on being a better dad and husband, and secondly, on helping others. And who better to help than his fellow hockey enforcers. He knew what they were going through. He had real-life experience with the depression and anxiety, the anger and the rage.

Dale signed on to a proposed class-action lawsuit with more than 100 other players, including former all-stars Bernie Nicholls, Gary Leeman, and Dave Christian. They were suing the NHL for allegedly failing to protect or educate its players despite the fact that the league ought to have known about the link between repeated concussions and traumatic brain injuries.

The lawsuit made headlines across North America and even captured the attention of some high-profile politicians in Washington, DC. In autumn 2016, Purinton joined former NHL fighter Dan LaCouture and Paul Montador, the father of deceased former player Steve Montador, who died in 2015 and was later diagnosed with CTE, in a meeting with prominent representatives, including Connecticut senator Richard Blumenthal and Illinois congresswoman Jan Schakowsky.

Dale said it was anything but a love-in. He faced serious questions from the politicians as they sought to learn more about the hockey fighter's experience with traumatic brain injuries.

"When I was in Washington, I think a tough question for me was 'If you know all this stuff can happen, and all your friends are sick and people are dying [and have] addictions, why would you allow your kids to play?'" Purinton said. "And my answer to that is: I love the NHL, it gave me an amazing life, and it gave me pretty much everything I have. But it also gave me a lot of terrible things. I just want some of the rules changed. So if we can change these rules, it starts from the top, then it comes through minor hockey, then my kids can play this amazing game and have this amazing experience without risking these injuries."

Even when Dale speaks truth to power in the hockey world, he wants to ensure that his sincere love for the game is fully understood. "I love hockey, man. I absolutely live for it," he said passionately. "I hate that people are getting sick, that people are living on the streets, that people have voices in their heads. This isn't just a coincidence. This shit's real, and this is happening because of these rules."

Following the meetings in Washington, four ranking Democratic members from the congressional Committee on Energy and Commerce sent a letter to NHL commissioner Gary Bettman. It asked Bettman to answer seven questions on subjects including new details of the league's concussion protocol, plans to limit fighting and hits to the head, and the outreach work the NHL does in communicating the dangers of playing hockey, even at the minor hockey level.

Bettman responded with a fifteen-page letter. The commissioner leaned heavily on the tried-and-tested argument that fights are actually required to police the game and protect smaller, more skilled players.

Congresswoman Schakowsky was unimpressed by the league's response, telling the *Hockey News* Bettman sounded "a little bit like the tobacco industry," in his denial of the reality that many players were suffering from traumatic brain injuries.

And Purinton wasn't just networking and advocating on the political level. He was also trying to recruit more players to the class-action lawsuit. He was calling old teammates and letting them know what was going on and how they could be a part of it. The uptake was slow, and Dale felt like some of the people he was counting on were letting him down.

When Dale spoke about the players who failed to support the concussion lawsuit, it was the first and only time over the course of our interviews that he showed any sign of anger. His gait sped up, and his voice rose ever so slightly.

Hockey fighters live by a code, and a big part of that code is standing up for your teammates. So it's easy to understand why he felt such a visceral sense of betrayal. In his mind, teammates are supposed to stand up for one another, and in this case, so many of them haven't.

"It's 2018, grab your balls," he said sternly. "We're supposed to be warriors. We're teammates, and when it comes down to it, you're just an individual, self-survival, you know? People, they just don't give a shit. Until it directly affects you."

The specific source of Purinton's anger within our conversation was Hockey Hall of Famer Eric Lindros, one of his teammates in New York. At one time, Lindros was an unstoppable physical force on the ice. He instilled fear in his opponents with his crushing checks, raw speed, and skill. After a few years, though, Lindros became the poster boy for the devastating impact of concussions. The former Flyers captain famously took a number of egregiously dirty elbows to the head from Devils defenseman Scott Stevens. These are the kinds of hits that change not only a player's skill but his life altogether. After so many head injuries, Lindros was never the same. He was still a mountain of a man, but he couldn't use his body in the same punishing way as when he took the league by force early in his career.

From Dale's perspective, if anyone would understand the lawsuit against the NHL, it would have to be Lindros. But he was wrong. Lindros wouldn't sign up for the class action.

While Purinton's rant may have been spurred by our conversation about Lindros, it was directed at all the players who declined to join. "If it was your son, or your brother, or your family member who killed himself or was living on the street, you'd probably be looking at it a little different," he said. "But when it doesn't directly affect you, you might just say, 'That's a guy I know, one of my old teammates, but fuck, I got my own life to worry about.' You just kind of move on."

Despite Purinton's efforts, the class-action lawsuit against the NHL proved to be fruitless. Instead of rule changes and some financial compensation, the players got only further frustration and uncertainty. In July 2018, US district judge Susan Nelson wrote a forty-six-page decision that acknowledged similarities in the players' cases and some valid reasons for suing as a class, but in the end, she opined that "widespread differences in applicable state laws" when it came to the medical monitoring the players wanted would cause significant case management difficulties.[17] The class action was dead.

But lawyers continued to work with the NHL behind the scenes, and on November 12, 2018, a tentative non-class deal was announced between the players and the league. Let's just say the deal fell short of the National Football League's billion-dollar settlement for a similar lawsuit. The NHL accepted zero liability for injuries to the players.

It agreed to pay $18.9 million to the 318 players in the suit. Players opting in to the deal became eligible for a $22,000 payout. There was a medical component too, with players who tested positive twice or more receiving neurological testing and assessment worth up to $75,000. And finally, the NHL agreed to establish a Common Good Fund of $2.5 million for players in need after their playing days are over. Twenty-two grand and some medical testing for a potential lifetime of pain from traumatic brain injuries.

Dale Purinton, like many of the players involved in the suit, found the offer insulting. In fact, he still hasn't ruled out taking on the NHL in a lawsuit of his own. "It's not even a personal gain," he said. "I more just want people to be aware of what's going on and to find other guys help. And I think, by doing so, I would get stuff out of that too, right?"

On the surface, Dale Purinton has sketched out a pretty good post-hockey, post-prison life for himself. He's back in Shawnigan Lake, where he works in the forestry industry and coaches his oldest kid's hockey team. He's sober and attends regular meetings at a local treatment centre. He sometimes even gives inspirational speeches in the community, warning about the dangers of drugs and alcohol. Dale still hopes to help his fellow enforcers and does when he can. But he also needs help.

There's a lot of darkness in Purinton's life. And that darkness visits at unexpected times, in unexpected ways. Sadly, that seems to be a devastating pattern for so many former hockey fighters.

When Dale initially contacted me after reading the CBC Stephen Peat story, he made himself readily available for interviews and casual check-ins. He was quick to answer his phone, and if I left him a message, he'd call back the same day. When I asked him about being featured in this book, he said he was happy to help and immediately committed.

But in the summer of 2018, he went silent. I sent him a couple of texts each week. I called his cellphone, I tried his home phone number, and I even reached out to his wife on social media. I was coming up empty, and the silence continued for about three months.

I was beginning to wonder what was going on with Dale. Maybe he'd taken the family on a long summer holiday. Maybe he changed phones. Maybe he just didn't want to talk to me anymore. But I had a hunch things weren't going so well, and it turned out that feeling was right on the money. Dale was dealing with a long stretch of bad mental health. His depression and anxiety had been dogging him for weeks.

"There was a couple days this summer I couldn't even go outside," he explained when we finally reconnected. "I couldn't leave the place until it got dark out. I do get sad lots, and as much work as I put in, I still suffer ... Something's always going on ... I still suffer from sadness, and anxiety. This isn't just a coincidence, man." Purinton strongly believes that his struggles stem from his life as a hockey enforcer.

And he's not only dealing with depression and anxiety. Dale says his emotional state has become almost permanently unstable and fragile, to the point where seemingly harmless things can send him into a spiral. "I'll read, like, a birthday card at [the drugstore]," he said. "And I'll have an emotional breakdown in the aisle, just bawling. I struggled all summer. That's why I didn't get ahold of you."

Compounding his current difficulties is the fact that Purinton's no longer living at home with his wife and kids. This time, it was his decision to leave. It's a decision he still seems to be grappling with.

As our series of emotionally charged interviews came to a close,

I asked Dale the big question I'd also asked James McEwan and Stephen Peat: Does he think he has chronic traumatic encephalopathy?

"I don't think so," he answered. "My wife would disagree. But I definitely have some sort of damage. I'm just emotionally unstable. I get clouds over me a little bit, like I got depression. I go for weeks where I'm just in a super sad mood and there's nothing I can do about it. So it's really up and down, and I'm sure I'm hard to be around."

Our final conversation ended the same way it began: with Dale expressing his deep concern for the plight of his fellow hockey fighters. His worry is not so much for himself but for others. We once again talk about his friend Stephen Peat. Purinton passionately defends Stephen and any other former enforcer who is struggling. That's the kind of guy Dale has become. For him, it now always comes back to his concern for other people.

"It's tough for me to move on, and that's why I always try to contact the guys because it's like, man, I could be in that same situation at any time," he said. "And the reality is, how far are we from that? One step, I could be living on the streets. And that's the reality. I don't fake it. I don't skirt the issue, it's the reality of it. I think it's possible for anyone. I don't think six years ago anyone thought Stephen Peat would be living on the streets."

Dale ended with a passionate plea. He told me about the changes he wants to see to avoid more human destruction. He wants former fighters taken care of. He wants the NHL to step up and show some compassion. He wants to clean up the game he loves, to minimize the violence so that his kids can enjoy it, like he did but without the injuries and the pain and the devastation.

"These are unbelievable humans that are playing that game," Purinton told me. "And as soon as they're done, some of them are sick and [the NHL] just throws them to the waste. Stephen Peat and

Matt Johnson and Joe Murphy should not be living in the streets. All those guys that passed away should not have. They should be with us today. And we should be helping them. These are all guys that are productive, they sold out your buildings before, they have so much more to give and so much more to offer. They could be around coaching and teaching kids in organizations, public speaking, but they're no longer with us, man. These are amazing humans."

Dale Purinton's lament is one of pain and regret. And he's taken that pain and that regret and pragmatically repackaged them. He's internalized them and expunged them in the form of hope. That hope is for those who fought before and for those who fight still. It's for his kids and the other players he coaches. And although he so often focuses on others who struggle in their post-fighting careers, he has hope for himself too.

Dale Purinton is on a journey. He's on a quest for atonement. Atonement for the dirty hits and for the injuries he handed out in abundance. For the drugs and for the alcohol that clouded his vision for so long. For that horrible moment on the cabin steps in New York. For letting down his young family when they needed their dad.

Only in elevating his fellow warriors when they're at their lowest can Purinton likewise elevate himself. This pursuit, along with his day-to-day struggles, is Dale's penance. He's surviving, and trying to help others do the same. The path may seem straightforward, but it's anything but easy. It's a struggle. After all these years, this son of a hockey tough guy, this brother of nine, this enforcer, this cheap-shot artist, this father, this advocate, continues to fight in more ways than one. And there's no end in sight.

CHAPTER 12

WHY WE TEACH KIDS TO FIGHT ON ICE

And now our first scrap ... Hey, it's Kaid Oliver again, roughin' it up
with Riley Stadel. A sixteen-year-old versus a twenty-year-old here ...
a pretty spirited scrap, Oliver holding his own, but then the veteran
gets the final say in that one. Good for Kaid Oliver, sixteen years old!
—Kaid Oliver vs. Riley Stadel
(Victoria Royals vs. Kelowna Rockets, October 26, 2016)

I HAVE two young kids. Maybe you do too. Maybe you have grandkids. Perhaps you have nieces or nephews. Possibly you're a teacher, or a coach, with kids in your care.

Picture those kids and think about all the amazing things you can show them in this world. You can teach them to read. You can show them how to walk, how to climb, how to ride a bike. You can teach them to skate, to pass, to shoot, to stickhandle. You can teach them about teamwork, togetherness, and friendship. You can show them kindness, and belonging. You can (and must) show them love.

But the hockey world is different. Because along with many of those aforementioned jewels of the human condition, some parents choose to teach their kids how to fight. With bare hands. On ice.

When I look at my kids, and the joy and innocence and curiosity with which they approach the world, I can't possibly fathom teaching them to fight another child. It's antithetical to everything I love about being a parent. And it just doesn't seem right.

But let's slow our roll on the judgment for just a second here. Let's walk a mile in these parents' shoes, and put the lovey-dovey stuff aside for a moment.

Now, imagine your kid is twelve, thirteen, fourteen years old and he's pretty damn good on the ice. Maybe your boy's playing

AAA hockey, and he's faster, stronger, and more skilled than most of his competition. Major junior scouts are starting to show up at his games. Maybe they've told you that your son will be drafted.

When big-time junior hockey becomes a probable path for your kid, it changes the equation. The moral ground that once seemed so stable becomes a lot shakier. In fact, things start to tilt quickly in the opposite direction and the math starts to look pretty straightforward.

If your kid's going to play junior hockey, and in junior hockey there are bare-knuckle fights, you'd better believe most parents are going to want their kids to know how to protect themselves in a scrap. Furthermore, when you consider that your fifteen- or sixteen-year-old might end up going toe to toe with a twenty-year-old man, you quickly realize that it's much less a choice than it is an imperative. It becomes a question of survival for your child.

So you've made up your mind. Your kid *must* learn how to fight before he ends up taking a vicious beatdown at the hands of a fully developed player, four to five years his senior. How do you do it?

The answer is pretty simple: you send him to a boxing gym.

I called a bunch of boxing gyms in the Vancouver area and discovered all of them had trained young hockey players to fight at some point. One trainer told me he was in the midst of training a thirteen-year-old who hoped to play junior hockey in the next couple of years.

In my many conversations with boxing trainers, none of them had any sense that teaching young hockey players to fight was unusual. I had anticipated that some of them might be a bit cagey about training such young kids to bare-knuckle box. I was wrong. There was no trepidation whatsoever.

I went to Diaz Combat Sports in East Vancouver to speak with owner, head instructor, and former MMA champion Ryan "the Lion"

Diaz. He told me he had trained members of the WHL's Vancouver Giants in the past. As the hip-hop music blared, leather gloves pounded heavy bags, and trainers raised their voices, pushing their fighters for that extra bit of effort, Diaz told me that training for hockey fighting isn't all that different from other combat sports.

"MMA's very similar to hockey fighting in the aspect of the close-quarter combat and the clinch because obviously when you're hockey fighting, you're clinching," Diaz said. "There's tricks you can do in the clinch, like pulling and punching, and then figure out ways to manipulate the jersey, 'cause that's a lot like jiu-jitsu with the gi, right?" (The gi is the uniform for jiu-jitsu, a Brazilian martial art that focuses on grappling.)

Although it may look like hockey fights consist solely of two big dudes throwing heavy haymakers on repeat, Diaz says that's simply not the case. There's (usually) a lot more nuance. "You have to understand to watch the grip," Diaz told me. "When they start getting into the jostling, they're grabbing that jersey. When you grab that jersey, you're handicapped for certain things."

Diaz puts his left hand on my shoulder, and pulls, hockey-scrap style. "If I grab you on that arm, you can't use that arm to punch me now," he said. "If I pull the jersey above your head, you can't see. So it does change the game a bit with that jersey. People don't understand it's not just swinging, swinging, swinging."

As Diaz wraps up our brief but enlightening hockey-fighting workshop, he makes an important point. He tells me that for the Vancouver Giants who trained in boxing and MMA it wasn't so much about fighting. It was about confidence.

"I want to set the record straight ... They didn't come here to fight," Diaz asserted. "The Giants didn't call me and say, 'Hey, Ryan, I want you to teach my guys to fight.' It was actually for the young guys to gain the confidence, to know that, 'Hey, if I had to fight, I could fight."

Every single person I spoke to—players, coaches, and boxing trainers—insisted that the goal of training in combat sports is not necessarily to gain proficiency as a fighter but rather to build mental fortitude and preparedness in the face of the objective reality of hockey fighting.

On the one hand, it makes sense. A player's confidence in their ability to play a high-impact, full-contact sport would almost certainly increase knowing that the bigger, tougher players on the other team couldn't steamroll them with physicality and fisticuffs. But on the other hand, it's kind of a chicken-and-egg argument. If young players didn't learn to fight, perhaps there would be fewer fights and players wouldn't need the training in the first place.

John Ludvig is a young player who learned how to box, and to box well. The native of Kamloops, BC, fought seven times during his rookie year with the Portland Winterhawks at the age of seventeen. He told me he'd been training at boxing gyms since he was a little kid.

"I'm not going out looking for fights, definitely not," Ludvig said. "But when I know someone on the other team is trying to scare our guys, or intimidate guys on our team, then I can go out there and change that right away."

That boxing experience means John feels entirely comfortable dropping the gloves. "I have full confidence in myself," he stated, straddling the line of cockiness. "When I go into a fight, I'm never going in nervous or scared or stuff. Basically, when I go up to a guy and let him know, 'You can't be doing that' and I'm going to drop the gloves with him and he's got to stand up for himself ... I just like that part that I can stick up for me and my teammates."

Nick Martino, of Griffins Boxing & Fitness in North Vancouver, BC, is another boxing coach who has regularly trained hockey players headed for junior. He echoed Ryan Diaz's belief that fostering confidence in young players takes precedence over the actual fighting.

But when it comes to that fight training, Nick focuses on possibly the most unique aspect of hockey scraps: the fact that the combatants are on skates. In no other form of pugilism are the competitors so starved for balance. "Part of the training is a lot of off-balance drills," Martino told me. "To actually get comfortable being in an off-balance position so they can actually throw punches when they're not really in balance."

Hockey fights don't last all that long, which also informs Martino's training. "What I usually tell them to do is, basically, get in there right away, grab the jersey, and go. Be the first one," Nick explained. "Because in a hockey fight, they're not very long. You're not doing, like, three-minute rounds here. When you're doing a hockey fight, you're lucky if you get even a minute. So it's basically who gets in there first and delivers the first few shots and actually gets the advantage."

And it's not just the boxing coaches who train young hockey players to fight. Tim Preston, head coach of Impact Hockey Development in Langley, believes that, as a matter of principle, players moving up to the junior level should learn how to protect themselves. The former WHL standout with the Seattle Thunderbirds and draft pick of the Buffalo Sabres prides himself on preparing kids to reach that elite level of play.

Preston feels he wouldn't be doing his job if he didn't prime the players for the reality of fighting. "I try to teach the players how to protect themselves, how to be aware, how to understand what to do if that does happen," he said. "The most important thing is making sure you take care of yourself, protecting yourself. And just showing the players little tips and little things what to do, how to hold on and how to tie a guy's jersey up and things like that."

Tim is adamant that the very last thing he wants is his young players skating around looking for a fight. But again, for this coach and so many others, it comes down to a bare-bones pragmatism: What if there is a fight? Will my player know what to do? Will he be safe? And there's also the question for a young player trying to make an impression at his first junior hockey tryout: What do the coaches want to see?

"We don't want players to go out there and fight," Preston said. "We just know that it's still a reality in the game. When you do go to a camp it's very, very competitive, and a lot of times you don't have a lot of time to showcase what you can do, so if you have an opportunity to show that you have courage, and you can show that you're not going to back down and you're not afraid, then I think it's important to understand how to protect yourself. Kids come into our camp all the time in the summer and they ask us stuff like, 'Okay, if I was to get into a fight, what would I do? How do I make sure I tie a guy up?' and we just show them those things."

As Preston and I discussed his hockey-fighting ethos rinkside, the conversation became a bit more complicated. Tim is not just a hockey coach. He's also a hockey dad. And at the time of our interview, his sixteen-year-old son, Carson, was only months removed from his first junior camp with the Seattle Thunderbirds, where as you might expect, the play out on the ice got a bit chippy.

"I was in a battle down low and one of my teammates took the puck and shot it on net and all of us, we went to the net and we were poking at the puck trying to get a rebound," Carson explained to me. "The play stopped and someone came up to me and said, 'Hey, get out of here,' and I'm like, 'What are you going to do?' and it kind of escalated a bit."

Carson, only five-seven, had been in countless scrums in front of the net throughout his minor hockey career, but he'd never been in a legitimate gloves-off, bare-knuckle fight. Until then, he'd always had a full face mask to protect him. But this was different. All eyes were on him as he confronted the player vying for that same vaunted spot on the Thunderbirds' roster. The harsh reality of hockey fighting was laid bare before him.

"One of my teammates dropped the gloves and I thought to myself, 'Well, maybe if he's doing it, should I do it too?'" Carson reflected. "It didn't really get to that point, but we kind of all sat back and watched him."

The tension dissipated for Carson. First fight averted for the time being.

So what was it like for Tim watching his son toe the precipice of a real-deal hockey scrap?

"As a parent, you want your kid to be safe," Preston said. "And so if Carson was to get into a fight, you know, I'd be nervous for him because I'd think, 'Okay, you got to protect yourself, like don't hurt yourself' and all that. And same for the other person, you don't want to see them get hurt as well. But also, too, maybe there might be a part of you that thinks, 'You know what, good for you, you stood your ground, and you showed the players on the ice and the coaches and the scouts and everybody that you're not afraid and that you'll stand up for yourself, and that you might not be a fighter, but if something comes up, you're not going to back down.'"

I spoke to three other young players in the Western Hockey League about learning to fight in order to thrive and survive as they climb the elite hockey ranks. All of them were eighteen or younger, children in the eyes of the law. None was allowed to drink legally, and only one was allowed to vote. But that didn't stop them from bare-knuckle boxing at mid-ice on the regular.

Riley McKay is a rugged forward from Swan River, Manitoba. As a member of the Spokane Chiefs, he led the WHL in fights three years in a row (2016–19). Riley is clear on his role and has no delusions of grandeur. He's on the ice for one purpose, and that is to police and patrol the game. If an opponent steps out of line and takes a shot, clean or otherwise, at his team's most skilled players, Riley steps in.

"I like to play a physical role, getting in on pucks, making sure guys are safe out there, and not letting anyone touch our star players," McKay said. "It's unreal and, you know, getting all the fans cheering and all the adrenaline you get, you really can't feel anything. But it gets your team going, gets the guys going, it gives you energy ... so I think it's great for the game."

For McKay, and most fighters, instinct takes over when the gloves hit the ice. There's really no time to think about strategy and approach. "You just kind of act, but mostly I try not to get hit." He laughed. "That's what's going through my head. Usually, I just try to get the helmet off of him first so when I'm throwing punches, I'm not busting up my hand on his helmet. It feels great, you know, it gets the guys going, they're cheering on the bench, the fans are going pretty crazy, it really energizes the whole game."

I asked Riley, as someone who has already fought dozens of times before turning twenty years old, whether he ever thinks about the potential dangers of traumatic brain injuries.

The short answer: not particularly.

"I haven't had any problems before, so I haven't been too worried about it," he responded nonchalantly. "But obviously if I take a good punch to the head, I kind of am like, 'Okay, am I okay to finish the game?' ... But no, I've held up pretty strong. I must have a pretty hard noggin because I haven't been injured yet."

Kaid Oliver has been in his fair share of scraps, too, but unlike Riley, he's not an enforcer. Far from it. The hard-nosed forward prides himself on a physical style of play. And Kaid is well aware that with the physicality he brings to the Victoria Royals comes the likelihood of fisticuffs. He's fought twelve times in his young major junior career. But he insists, "It isn't that I'm going out there looking to fight ... it's if I hit someone, someone might come over and things happen, right? Most of my fights have come from playing a physical style of game and people get pissed off about it. You kind of have to stand up as a younger guy in the league and prove that you're not going to back down to people."

Kaid told me that the injuries commonly associated with fighting don't worry him, especially compared to the other risks that come with stepping onto the ice. "It's a hand coming at you. It doesn't have too much force," Oliver said. "When you punch, it's mostly coming from your hips, so it doesn't have that much power. I'm more worried, for concussions, it would probably be getting [bodychecked] or something. Fighting, you can defend yourself. If you're defending yourself, then you shouldn't have a problem."

And just like his young fighting counterparts, John Ludvig bristled when I asked him about head injuries and the possibility of facing the grim reality of CTE. "No, I haven't [thought about that] before," Ludvig said. "I go into the fight not thinking about any of that. That stuff rarely happens, but if it does, it's awful to see, but I haven't ever thought of it when I'm going in."

While it's mostly unsurprising that young talented athletes pursuing their pro hockey dreams aren't sidetracked by the thought of possible brain injuries inherent to fighting, it was also clear from my discussions with them that their knowledge of the potential devastation was lacking. Or maybe, in their dogged pursuit of a dream, they've been forced to park those concerns, and any related curiosity, in order to continue that quest, no matter the consequences.

When it comes to NHL enforcers, there hasn't been one much bigger, much tougher, or with a more punishing left hand than Georges Laraque. Laraque racked up more than 140 fights and 1,126 penalty minutes playing for the Edmonton Oilers, Montreal Canadiens, Pittsburgh Penguins, and Arizona Coyotes. He also scored fifty-three goals.

Laraque has unique insight into the mindset of a junior hockey tough guy: "When I played junior hockey I fought a bit," Georges began. "But first of all, I never wanted to be a fighter, I did it 'cause I thought I had to to be in the NHL. But everybody wants to be in the NHL with their talent. So if there's no fighting in junior hockey, you're going to focus on your skill ... because first and foremost the goal of playing hockey is actually to skate and score and to be part of the line and to play regularly."

The Montreal native is happy to see staged fights mostly out of the sport, and he supports eliminating fighting from the junior level. But don't get the wrong idea. Laraque still very much supports fighting in the professional game. He believes it's an imperative for entertainment and safety.

"Fighting has been part of the NHL from the beginning because hockey is an emotional sport and physicalness [sic] was always part of the game," he said. "The fact that the NHL has cleaned it up to make sure there isn't guys anymore that are only there for [fighting], and now they want guys that can also play the game, and if a fight happens, it's not premeditated, that's good. When you're in it and you're making a career out of it and you're going to be a physical guy that can still play the game but has to fight sometimes, this is something that I'm totally up for. That has to stay in the game."

The hulking former forward believes that fighting is not actually doing much of the damage when it comes to traumatic brain injuries. Laraque points to hits to the head and even the de facto removal of the red line and the two-line pass rule as culprits of rising rates of concussions. Laraque explained that, in removing the hindrance of the red line at centre ice, there's no reason for a player to slow down, and they're able to pick up more speed than ever. Laraque correctly pointed out that a collision at top speed means that, even if the head is not directly struck, the force and possible whiplash can still lead to an injured brain.

Georges also echoed the argument, heard earlier in this chapter, that a punch thrown on skates isn't really a serious punch at all. (Watch one of Laraque's many fights and you might beg to differ.)

"When you fight in hockey, the punch you get to somebody's head, it's not a full-blown punch like when you're in boxing or something," Laraque argued. "When you're on skates, you're out of balance and it's really rare [to seriously injure someone]."

When I asked if he'd ever experienced any devastating challenges like James McEwan, Stephen Peat, Dale Purinton, or Wade Belak, Rick Rypien, and Derek Boogaard, Laraque's tone softened a bit. (Laraque fought Belak six times, Boogaard three times in 2005–06 alone, and Purinton as well.) He quickly said no but didn't answer the question directly either.

"I feel very fortunate that, you know, I never took any drugs, any steroids or anything like that, and I wasn't drinking alcohol," he said, sounding contemplative. "I feel blessed I was really lucky the way that I did the job. And I consider myself lucky that I did not play in those days where there was way more tough guys, there was a line of tough guys per team, because it was way tougher."

It's interesting that Laraque supports fighting in the pros but also supports taking it out of junior. In my dozens of interviews with major junior players, coaches, and owners, it was clear that the major junior leagues consider themselves to be bona fide training grounds for professional hockey. And as the thinking goes, if there's fighting in the NHL, players in major junior need to be prepared for that eventuality.

But with fighting way down in the NHL, the numbers in the WHL haven't quite followed suit. Fights are down sixty-five percent over ten years and seventy-six percent over twenty years in the Dub, but the decrease hasn't kept pace with the NHL's, and the overall numbers are still much higher.

Over the past ten years in the WHL, fights have occurred at nearly double the rate (ninety-four percent more) as they do in the NHL. In the past ten years referees have handed out 11,359 fighting majors in the WHL compared to 8,640 in the NHL (remember that the NHL has more teams and games to account for). And even in the Ontario Hockey League (OHL), where fighting happens significantly less, the boys still fight way more than the men. Over the past ten years, fights have happened fifty-six percent more often in the OHL than in the NHL.

But despite that ongoing trend of the juniors out-fighting the pros, Laraque doesn't think prohibiting fighting is necessary or even useful, pointing to former Anaheim Ducks tough guy George Parros as an example. Parros played four years of National Collegiate Athletic Association (NCAA) hockey at Princeton University before cracking a professional roster. Because NCAA players wear full face masks, fighting is exceedingly rare. Laraque's argument is that Parros, one of the most fearsome players of his generation, only needed to learn to fight once he reached the American Hockey League. (Parros actually played a year of junior hockey before NCAA in the North American Hockey League, where he dabbled in fisticuffs.)

But the very fact that fighting is accepted in hockey, especially in the junior ranks, means kids, parents, trainers, and coaches must change the way they train and change the way they think about the game. In the end, it means they must shift their focus away from skating, shooting, passing, and puck handling toward combat. Or at least survival in the face of combat.

Fighting's existence in hockey is an all-or-nothing proposition when it comes to the impact it has on the kids who feel they *must* learn to fight. That they must learn to defend themselves against bigger, stronger players who, unlike them, are fully developed adults. That they must learn to deliver powerful blows to the head and face of their opponents. That they must learn to receive those same powerful punches to their own head and face. That blows to the brain, and the consequences that come with them, are simply part and parcel of pursuing the game they love.

When you sign your kid up to play hockey, you're signing them up for all kinds of beautiful moments: goals, wins, life lessons, friendships, and more. But if your kid has any inclination toward that Canadian dream of playing hockey at the highest level, you're also signing them up to fight, whether you like it or not.

For young elite players, fighting is as inherent to hockey as a slash to the back of the knees or a good clean bodycheck. You simply have to accept that these things happen in the sport, and if you're the one doling out the pain, all the better.

And those same young players know from Georges Laraque and other big-time pros that there's a handsome living to be made in pro hockey, even for the less-skilled players. Laraque, and so many others, have proven that untold millions can be yours if you're willing to make up for your shortcomings with a lot of grit, heart, and a willingness to sacrifice your body. If what it takes is a whole lot of physical play and a few fights to grab some attention and make a name for yourself, so be it.

For Georges, fighting was his calling card. It was a ticket to fame and prosperity. He reportedly earned more than US$10.6 million over the course of his career. That's a whole lot of dough. It would take the median Canadian household 198 years to make that much money.[18]

So if you can look back at your career, free of major injuries, and see all those zeros in your bank account, and look at the opportunities afforded to you by fighting in the biggest hockey league in the world, it only makes sense that you would support a practice that enriched you so thoroughly.

Hockey fighting is like playing a high-stakes lottery. If you come out on top, that could mean fame, adulation, and millions of dollars. But if you lose, the results can be disastrous and even deadly.

WHAT NEEDS TO HAPPEN

I ask you to sit down and turn your back to these fights.
—James McEwan

MANY OF the people I interviewed for this book were quick to point out that fighting is fading from the game. The so-called staged fights featuring two supposedly skill-less goons have gone, and all that remains are anger-fuelled skirmishes between skilled players when tempers have simply flared up.

Proponents argue that the fighting that remains provides a necessary release valve for a game that is unique in its physicality and tight confines. And although it's objectively true that the number of fights in the NHL and junior hockey has decreased in recent years, the fact that fighting exists at all, that it's permitted and tolerated, has an extraordinary impact on the way the game is played, the people who play it, and how they pursue hockey mastery and professionalism.

The reality of the issue is, that when you speak to the James McEwans, the Stephen Peats, and the Dale Purintons, the players who have faced massive struggles in the years following their hockey careers, you can understand why they, their friends, and their families see fighting as a harmful force in the game of hockey. The players have lived with the headaches, boiled over with rage, and faced down depression, anxiety, and suicide. Their loved ones have experienced the empty feeling of helplessness that comes with witnessing that pain and not knowing what to do about it.

In a way, it's almost like gun violence, or the opioid crisis, or a rare, incurable disease. Until you've experienced something so noxious first-hand, it's not something you can properly understand.

It's not something you've been forced to process and integrate into your life. That pain and devastation is unknowable because, quite simply, you haven't lived it. And to be fair, if you haven't lived it, how could you understand?

Therefore, the lack of understanding and continuing support for fighting, from people in this book and around the hockey world, is comprehensible if not entirely rational.

The truth is, James McEwan, Stephen Peat, and Dale Purinton have been through a lot. They feverishly pursued their hockey dreams by bare-knuckle boxing their way to the professional levels. And after the games were over, the crowds went home, the rinks went silent, and they hung up their skates, our three players were left with complicated lives filled with a lot of pain and suffering.

But despite what the sport took from them, and the pain it inflicted, somehow, they still love it. They love the game of hockey.

And that might be the most powerful testament to hockey of all. These men still revere the game that filled their lives with questions, fear, and pain. It may be hard to believe, but James and Dale still want to take part in the hockey world. They still want to feel the ice beneath their skates and the cold air on their faces. They want to pass along what they've learned to the next generation. Hockey's in their blood. It's the air they breathe. Hockey makes everything seem like it's going to be okay.

Dale continues to coach his kids in minor hockey. James has organized a unique hockey camp that integrates meditation and wellness into the training regimen. He's even talked about opening a healing centre for hockey players who have just ended their professional careers and might be searching for a new path.

Because of their injuries, but also because of their continuing passion for the game, James and Dale have thought long and hard about how hockey should change. They want to see the sport evolve so that the next generation of players (Dale's kids included) can enjoy the thrills and the joys the game has to offer without the breathtaking devastation that can come from the violence.

According to McEwan, some significant but easy rule changes would go a long way toward ending the fights. He wants to see bigger ice surfaces, fewer hits to the head, and larger fines and suspensions for players who fight.

"They've been using the same ice for how many years? A hundred years?" McEwan asked rhetorically. "Look how much faster and bigger guys are now. With the technology and the training, guys are faster than they've ever been. It would be nice to see the ice get bigger, and that would limit some of the huge hits and some of the issues that come around with the intensity of all that energy in a small space. And upping the penalties, suspensions, fines too. It'll be tough to get used to, but it'll help."

Outside of the rule changes, McEwan thinks it really comes down, first and foremost, to the fans. The owners and the players certainly play a huge role, but to James, true change begins with the fans. McEwan argues that owners are in the game to make money, and if the seats at the arena are full, they're happy. So if there's a perception that fighting is helping fill those seats, owners will continue to allow it. But what happens if fans turn away from the fighting? That's where McEwan sees the real power and possibility for change.

He speaks directly to the millions of fans across the continent. "I ask you to have the honour and courage to stop cheering for fights," McEwan urges. "Your response and cheering helps give it life. I ask you to sit down and turn your back to these fights."

James believes the fans have the power to influence the elimination of fighting, but it's clear to him that the owners and hockey power-brokers are the ones who, even if they're forced into it, will have to make the final, culture-shifting decision in the form of bold and unequivocal change.

"Please help eliminate violence in hockey by making a stand," McEwan appeals to the owners. "Stop allowing this to happen by promoting it, rewarding it, praising it, and letting it happen with minimal penalties. Please protect our players and our children coming up."

And of course, there's the players. They, just like McEwan, Peat, and Purinton, have an undying passion for the game and want to play it in front of the biggest crowds, with the highest stakes, and while making the most money. McEwan wants young athletes to think differently. He wants them to be better educated and, in turn, more thoughtful about the consequences of head shots and fights. McEwan wants the players to consider their own fallibility, their own mortality. He wants CTE, and its devastating symptoms, to be commonly understood and respected.

"Please treat yourself, teammates, and members of the other team with respect and hold each other to high standards of moral value and sportsmanship," McEwan pleads. "You are warriors and have tremendous hearts and the impact you have on our world is tremendous, more than you can even fathom right now. Be a true warrior of courage and integrity and make a stand for honour, peace, and respect, be this on or off the ice."

In our conversations, Stephen Peat and I rarely spoke about hockey. There was too much going on in the foreground with his health and the law to discuss how to cure hockey's fighting problem, but I never heard him say a bad word about the sport itself, only some of the people in and around it.

Peat's father, Walter, made it clear that he would like to see some changes that would prevent future players from suffering injuries similar to his son's. "I think the NHL is trying to clean up its act, to cut back on the fighting and the violence," Walter said. "But at the end of the day, I think they realize that there's a thirst for the violence that's out there still. I think the fan base has to turn their back on the violence in the game before it stops."

And when I asked Walter about NHL owners and their inaction on fighting, he was at first upset, and then became philosophical about the logical gymnastics that are required to keep fighting in the game.

"How long have we been playing these games?" Walter wondered. "How many owners and how many years have they been in hockey and watching what's going on, and they still haven't learned that the violence ... they're condoning long-term and possibly fatal injuries to players. There's going to come a day where players will start getting killed in hockey, and I'm talking on the ice. You have bare-fisted fights that go on on the ice. What makes me think that society's lost it, is that you have two kids out on the street and they're bare-knuckle fighting and the police come along and throw them both in jail ... But society, the police, the government, and everybody endorse [fighting] because it's a hockey game."

Dale Purinton advocates for a completely different approach. He doesn't necessarily want to see fighting out of the game, but he does want to see the elimination of bodychecking, not just hits to the head. That's right, no more hitting in hockey, whatsoever.

"First we got to take hitting out of the game," Purinton said. "Maybe we got to bring the red line back and slow things down a bit. Maybe more of a clutch-and-grab style. Sidney Crosby, he's never had a concussion in a fight, but he's only one concussion away from losing his career, and it's not going to be because of a fight. [Most] concussions are from hits, bad hits. And constant banging.

And that's coming from a guy—I love to hit. I fricking loved it. It was my whole game."

Purinton isn't clinging to the fighting, but he does believe in policing the game. In the end, however, he seems fine to let it go. "I would keep fighting in because it makes people accountable," he told me. "I'm okay with fighting being taken out, but you got to take the worst thing out first and that's hitting. Hitting causes most of it. And then, if you want to look at fighting, then I'm okay with that. But we got to make it safe for these guys."

For Purinton, it's all about leaving the game better than he found it, particularly for his own boys.

From a medical perspective, the solution for fighting, and the potentially dire consequences that come with it, is putting an end to the repeated concussive and sub-concussive blows to the head. University of British Columbia neuroscientist Dr Naznin Virji-Babul says parents, coaches, and administrators need to stop the violence before it starts in minor hockey and carries on into junior. In other words, the adults need to step in. "We really need to go back to first principles in terms of why are we letting this happen?" she said. "Why are we tolerating this kind of action? We shouldn't be. The game can be played in a much cleaner way where we don't subject teenagers to these unnecessary risks that could have long-term effects on their brain function. We as adults, who are responsible for them, shouldn't be allowing this to happen."

There is one group of highly influential power-brokers that has yet to come up, and that's the sponsors. Look just behind two players going toe to toe along the boards and what do you see? The logos of the most influential corporations on the continent: Toyota, Pepsi, Coca-Cola, Ticketmaster, Tim Hortons, McDonald's, Verizon, Dunkin' Donuts, Geico, Air Canada, and many more. The biggest companies in the world pay to have their logos seen, yes, when the Sidney Crosbys and Alex Ovechkins score game-winning goals but also as blood splatters the ice in the midst of a bare-knuckle boxing match.

I interviewed a number of big Canadian sponsors about their marketing investments in hockey and how they feel about being featured alongside young men (teenagers, at the junior level) who are trying their best to beat the living daylights out of one another. The overarching message from those sponsors was that perhaps fighting wasn't their favourite part of the game, but they believed they had no role in influencing the way the sport of hockey is actually played. For them, hockey is an opportunity to connect with communities of fans in a place they love to be. If fighting is a part of that equation, so be it.

A representative from Canadian real estate giant RE/MAX told me in no uncertain terms that fighting is a part of hockey, and the fans and his company's customers understand that.

Meanwhile, Jean Whitaker, a former spokesperson for Canadian national restaurant chain Boston Pizza, explained that regulating the way the game is played is not the sponsors' job, but the more the conversation about fighting takes centre stage, the more companies are forced to consider its impact. "We go into it assuming that the teams and the players, they're being considered and their health is being considered by the league, so I don't think that would be on us," Whitaker said. "While we as a company and as a brand don't support or encourage violence in any way ... the more people talk about it, the more it becomes something we do think about, what does our sponsorship of this mean in terms of support of that kind of behaviour?"

So what kinds of rule changes might lead to less fighting on the ice? The most effective seem to be automatic and cascading suspensions for players who fight multiple times in a season.

For an excellent case study that illustrates just how effective these kinds of rule changes can be, we need look no further than the major junior OHL, arguably the top development league for the NHL.

Before its 2016–17 season, the league's board of governors decided to take a stronger stance against fighting by implementing an automatic suspension for any player who fought three times or more in a season. For a player's third fight, and every fight after that, he received a two-game suspension.

So what was the result? Simply put, the rule worked. Fighting plummeted. In the season prior, there had been 632 fighting majors, or a fight in forty-six percent of the league's games. In the season after the rule change, there were 335 fighting majors, or a fight in twenty-five percent of games. With one modest rule change, the OHL immediately cut fighting nearly in half. Regulation works.

But regulation or not, we know that fighting numbers are down across the board. Many of fighting's supporters, both hard-core and moderate, will tell you that the decreasing numbers in all leagues illustrate that staged fights (those where the sole purpose of an enforcer's shift is to drop the gloves as soon as the puck drops) are out of the game, and the only fights left are those inspired by real emotion. The kind where a real hockey player (many people bring up Jarome Iginla as an example) is pissed off enough to drop the gloves, to show toughness, and to help his team win the game. I find the differentiation between the two supposedly distinctive kinds of fights immaterial. The intent of the fight, or the emotions behind it, doesn't matter. In the end, it is two grown men bare-knuckle boxing each other, and causing potentially dangerous injuries.

I have to admit, in the midst of crunching the shrinking fighting numbers, I had a bit of a crisis of confidence. The numbers had decreased so much and so consistently that I began to experience a stinging sense of self-doubt. If fighting really is down this much, is the culture already accepting of these stories I'm telling and moving to address them? Is fighting slowly but surely becoming a thing of the past? Is this book really even necessary?

But that very night, I happened to have tickets to see the Vancouver Canucks take on the league-leading Tampa Bay Lightning at Rogers Arena in Vancouver. During the second period, all my doubts were immediately put to rest.

The period had no fewer than four fighting majors, along with seven roughing minors (many of which could easily have been ruled fighting majors) and a ten-minute misconduct penalty. The game was marred by sloppy, rough, and violent play that made it boring and difficult to watch. But the biggest cheers from the crowd, even compared with the response to the two Canucks goals, were for the fights. The crowd absolutely loved it.

The incessant violence came with a strong and troubling jux-taposition, too. As the referees continued to parade players to the penalty box, the jumbotron showed images of young children in the crowd. Although they were dancing to the music during the breaks in play, only moments before, they had witnessed, internalized, and normalized the sight of multiple grown adult men dropping their gloves to the ice and punching each other in the face. It was upsetting to consider that these hundreds of kids would go home, fall asleep, and wake up the next day for school with the idea that fighting like that is no big deal. That the only accountability for that kind of fighting is to sit in the box for five minutes, and then you're back doing what you love to do best.

I asked one of my seatmates, a woman in her mid-sixties, what she thought of the fights. She told me that the Canucks simply had to stand up for themselves, and she was glad they had done so. She was quick to clarify that, if she could have her way, fighting would be abolished all together, but as it is, if the refs won't call the game properly, the players have to take control. And that means fights.

The Canucks versus Lightning game was evidence that, no matter how much the fighting numbers plummet, as long as the violence is still allowed within the rules, it will not only survive but, on many nights, thrive.

Think back to when I criticized fighting on social media. Dismissiveness, name-calling, homophobia, sexism, and toxic masculinity ran rampant. When an issue like fighting in hockey becomes characterized by such extreme divisiveness, and becomes so deeply entrenched on each side of the issue, debate grinds to a halt. Each side of the argument knows what the other is going to say, and both feel as though nothing is going to change either way.

Fighting in hockey has come to be regarded as an unsolvable quagmire.

But the truth is that fighting is entirely solvable. All it requires is the will of hockey's power-brokers to make simple rule changes that would make fighting unpalatable for teams and players. With the help of McEwan and Purinton, I've laid out nearly a dozen possible fixes that could contribute to an eradication of fighting altogether. If we're honest, the fighting could be all but gone by tomorrow. And if not tomorrow, definitely before the beginning of next season. The more we pretend that solving the problems caused by hockey fighting is an intractable piece of unknowable rocket science, the longer it will pervade the sport. The longer children will witness bare-knuckle boxing on ice. The longer we'll see the long-term damage to humans who feel they need to fight to chase their dreams.

Hockey players are hockey players because they love to play the game. It's usually the thing they love to do most in the world. If players know that for fighting they'll receive not only heavy fines but also game misconducts followed by cascading suspensions, the fights will stop. The athletes simply will not repeatedly risk their most cherished ability to play the game, not to mention their livelihood.

Suspensions would shift the culture and send a clear message that this behaviour will not be tolerated. The number of fights would shrink quickly. And fighting in hockey would become first a rarity and then a distant memory.

Hockey is the sunrise. Hockey is the air we breathe. Hockey is the everflowing lifeblood.

It is played at every hour of the day, by every kind of person, on every kind of ice surface imaginable, in every corner of the continent. Hockey is everywhere. And for many, it is everything.

There is something so magnetic and so intrinsic about the sport of hockey that there are thousands of young people who are willing to do almost anything to pursue the sport at the highest level.

Maybe it's the money. Maybe it's the adulation. Maybe it's the thrill of trying to beat the odds. To prove everyone, including yourself, wrong.

Maybe it's delusion. Maybe it's unfulfilled ego. Maybe it's a lack of imagination.

But maybe it's simpler than all of that. Maybe it's a game that's so easy to fall in love with that nearly everyone who straps on skates and hits the ice wants to shoot, pass, and score to the best of their ability for as long as they possibly can.

Maybe hockey is now less a sport we play and more a part of who we are. It casts an intoxicating spell, and those who fall for it fall hard.

James McEwan, Stephen Peat, and Dale Purinton played hockey

because they loved it. But they also played because, for various but not dissimilar reasons, they had something to prove. They wanted to prove their value as people, to show those around them that they were worthy of attention, praise, and support. More than that, with their play on the ice, these young men wanted to show that they were deserving of love. Hockey was their passion, but it was also a vessel. It was the weapon they wielded to make their worth indisputable and inescapable. And, really, what better vessel than the game that everyone loves, that everyone reveres, that everyone stops what they're doing to sit down and watch on a Saturday night.

But to prove that worth and earn that love, and advance in the dog-eat-dog hockey world, they had to fight, with bare fists. They had to fight until their hands were broken and bloodied. Until their faces were bruised and gashed. Until their noses were broken and permanently deformed. Until their opponents crumbled to the ice. Until their brains were battered. Until their lives were devastated. Until they changed into entirely different people forever.

Forever. Forever. Hockey changed these men forever. McEwan, Peat, and Purinton are trying their very best to be okay. To live life. To be good people. To get by. To breathe and to exist. Like anyone else, they have good days and bad. Their post-hockey lives have been ongoing acts of defiance and of survival. Survival in the face of trauma. Their brains have been injured. Traumatized. Repeatedly. Forever. And ever.

It is that irreversible, undeniable foreverness that is missing from the hockey-fighting debate. We talk about toughness and identity and masculinity. We talk about history and tradition. We talk about momentum shifts, intimidation, and policing the game. We talk about children making a name for themselves. We talk about he who answers the bell and he who does not. For whom the bell tolls, forever and ever.

But what we don't talk about is the permanence of brain injury. The permanence of becoming an entirely new person. The permanence of facing death and either fighting back or succumbing to it. Permanence. Foreverness.

There are many in the hockey world who are ready to let fighting go. To leave the violence in the past and move forward with the speed and the skill and the beauty. But so many more cling to the fights. To them, fighting in hockey is primal. It's fundamental in its necessity. It's in their bones, even if they've never been, and never will be, in a hockey fight themselves.

To so many, fighting in hockey is a sacred rite. It is foundational to the sport, to the culture, and to the country.

It is belief. It is faith. It is religion.

But for that belief there is a severe human cost. The human cost of pain. Of sickness. Of loss. Of isolation. And of death.

These costs are inflicted because we not only allow but celebrate children, and then the men they become, for bare-knuckle boxing one another on ice. Those human costs are paid in the name of sport, in the name of passion, in the name of a great dream. In the name of hockey.

And once fighting is gone, it's true, hockey will never be the same. Because hockey will be less violent. Hockey will be safer. Hockey will be better.

NOTES

1. Dr Gabor Maté, "The Profound Power of an Amazonian Plant—and the Respect It Demands," Dr Gabor Maté, December 21, 2015, https://drgabormate.com/profound-power-amazonian-plant-respect-demands/.

2. Maté, "The Profound Power of an Amazonian Plant."

3. F. Palhano-Fontes, et al., "Rapid Antidepressant Effects of the Psychedelic Ayahuasca in Treatment-Resistant Depression: A Randomized Placebo-Controlled Trial," *Psychological Medicine* (March 2019): 655–63, https://www.ncbi.nlm.nih.gov/pubmed/29903051.

4. Oregon State Senate, Senate Committee on Workforce, Bill HB4093 A, Hearings before the Committee on Workforce, 79th Oregon Legislative Assembly, 2018, 4–5.

5. Sara Gelser, "Oregon State Senate Committee on Workforce Hearings," Senator Sara Gelser's testimony, February 27, 2018, video, 1:11:08, http://oregon.granicus.com/MediaPlayer.php?clip_id=24729.

6. Western Hockey League, "WHL Releases Independent Investigation Report on Oregon Senate Hearing Allegations," June 27, 2018, https://whl.ca/article/whl-releases-independent-investigation-report-on-oregon-senate-hearing-allegations.

7. *James Johnathon McEwan v. Canadian Hockey League, Western Hockey League, and Canadian Hockey Association*, Notice of Civil Claim, Supreme Court of British Columbia, January 9, 2019, https://www.courthousenews.com/wp-content/uploads/2019/01/Hockey.pdf.

8. Bennet Omalu, et al., "Postmortem Autopsy-Confirmation of Antemortem [F-18]FDDNP-PET Scans in a Football Player with Chronic Traumatic Encephalopathy," *Neurosurgery* 82, issue 2 (February 2018): 237–46, https://www.ncbi.nlm.nih.gov/pubmed/29136240.

9. BC Non-Profit Housing Association and M. Thomson Consulting, "2017 Homeless Count in Metro Vancouver," final report, September 2017, Metro Vancouver Homelessness Partnering Strategy Community Entity,

http://www.metrovancouver.org/services-regional-planning/homelessness/HomelessnessPublications/2017MetroVancouverHomelessCount.pdf.

10. "Victoria Rink," *Montreal Gazette*, March 3, 1875, 3.

11. "Hockey," *Montreal Evening Star*, March 4, 1875, 3.

12. "Canadian," *British Whig*, March 5, 1875, 2.

13. "Sports and Pastimes: Note and Comment," *Montreal Gazette*, January 20, 1886, 2.

14. All statistics regarding fighting in hockey are available online and updated regularly at https://www.hockeyfights.com.

15. House of Commons Subcommittee on Sports-Related Concussions, Hearings before the Subcommittee, Number 11, 1st session, 42nd parliament, May 1, 2019, https://www.ourcommons.ca/DocumentViewer/en/42-1/SCSC/meeting-11/evidence#Int-10589470.

16. *Jules Jobidon (appellant) v. Her Majesty the Queen (respondent)*, [1991] 2 S.C.R. 714, File No.: 21238, March 28, 1991, https://scc-csc.lexum.com/scc-csc/scc-csc/en/item/784/index.do.

17. Memorandum Opinion and Order in re: National Hockey League Players' Concussion Injury Litigation, United States District Court District of Minnesota. MDL No. 14-2551 (SRN/BRT), July 13, 2018, https://www.govinfo.gov/content/pkg/USCOURTS-mnd-0_14-md-02551/pdf/USCOURTS-mnd-0_14-md-02551-13.pdf.

18. Statistics Canada, "Household Income in Canada: Key Results from the 2016 Census," last updated September 27, 2017, https://www150.statcan.gc.ca/n1/daily-quotidien/170913/dq170913a-eng.htm.

BIBLIOGRAPHY

BC Non-Profit Housing Association and M. Thomson Consulting. "2017 Homeless Count in Metro Vancouver." Final report, September 2017. Metro Vancouver Homelessness Partnering Strategy Community Entity. http://www. metrovancouver.org/services/regional-planning/homelessness/ HomelessnessPublications/2017MetroVancouverHomelessCount. pdf.

"Canadian." *British Whig*, March 5, 1875.

Gelser, Sara. "Oregon State Senate Committee on Workforce Hearings." Senator Sara Gelser's testimony. February 27, 2018. Video, 1:11:08. http://oregon.granicus.com/MediaPlayer.php?clip_id=24729.

"Hockey." *Montreal Evening Star*, March 4, 1875.

Hockey Fights (database). www.hockeyfights.com/.

House of Commons Subcommittee on Sports-Related Concussions. Hearings before the Subcommittee. Number 11, 1st session, 42nd parliament, May 1, 2019. https://www.ourcommons.ca/Docu mentViewer/en/42-1/SCSC/meeting-11/evidence#Int-10589470.

James Johnathon McEwan v. Canadian Hockey League, Western Hockey League, and Canadian Hockey Association. Notice of Civil Claim. Supreme Court of British Columbia, January 9, 2019. https://www.courthousenews.com/wp-content/uploads/2019/01/ Hockey.pdf.

Jules Jobidon (appellant) v. Her Majesty the Queen (respondent). [1991] 2 S.C.R. 714, File No.: 21238, March 28, 1991. https:// scc-csc.lexum.com/scc-csc/scc-csc/en/item/784/index.do.

Maté, Gabor. "The Profound Power of an Amazonian Plant—and the Respect It Demands." Dr Gabor Maté. December 21, 2015. https://drgabormate.com/profound-power-amazonian-plant-respect-demands/.

Memorandum Opinion and Order in re: National Hockey League Players' Concussion Injury Litigation. United States District Court District of Minnesota. MDL No. 14-2551 (SRN/BRT), July 13, 2018. https://www.govinfo.gov/content/pkg/USCOURTS-mnd-0_14-md-02551/pdf/USCOURTS-mnd-0_14-md-02551-13.pdf.

Omalu, Bennet, Gary W. Small, Julian Bailes, Linda M. Ercoli, David A. Merrill, Koon-Pong Wong, Sung-Cheng Huang, Nagichettiar Satyamurthy, Jennifer L. Hammers, John Lee, Robert P. Fitzsimmons, and Jorge R. Barrio. "Postmortem Autopsy-Confirmation of Antemortem [F-18]FDDNP-PET Scans in a Football Player with Chronic Traumatic Encephalopathy." *Neurosurgery* 82, issue 2 (February 2018): 237–46. https://www.ncbi.nlm.nih.gov/pubmed/29136240.

Oregon State Senate. Senate Committee on Workforce. Bill HB4093 A. Hearings before the Committee on Workforce. 79th Oregon Legislative Assembly, 2018.

Palhano-Fontes, F., D. Barreto, H. Onias, K.C. Andrade, M.M. Novaes, J.A. Pessoa, S.A. Mota-Rolim, F.L. Osorio, R. Sanches, R.G. Dos Santos, L.F. Tofoli, G. de Oliveira Silveira, M. Yonamine, J. Riba, F.R. Santos, A.A. Silva-Junior, J.C. Alchieri, N.L. Galvao-Coelho, B. Lobao-Soares, J.E.C. Hallak, E. Arcoverde, J.P. Maia-de-Oliveira, and D.B. Araujo. "Rapid Antidepressant Effects of the Psychedelic Ayahuasca in Treatment-Resistant Depression: A Randomized Placebo-Controlled Trial." *Psychological Medicine* (March 2019): 655–63. https://www.ncbi.nlm.nih.gov/pubmed/29903051.

"Sports and Pastimes: Note and Comment." *Montreal Gazette*, January 20, 1886.

Statistics Canada. "Household Income in Canada: Key Results from the 2016 Census." Last updated September 27, 2017. https://www150.statcan.gc.ca/n1/daily-quotidien/170913/dq170913a-eng.htm.

"Victoria Rink." *Montreal Gazette*, March 3, 1875.

Western Hockey League. "WHL Releases Independent Investigation
Report on Oregon Senate Hearing Allegations." June 27, 2018.
https://whl.ca/article/whl-releases-independent-investigation-
report-on-oregon-senate-hearing-allegations.

ACKNOWLEDGMENTS

WRITING A book while raising two awesome kids and working full time at CBC Radio was a massive task, and I absolutely could not have done it without my partner, Sajeeda Kuthdoos. Not only did she provide support that allowed me the time to complete the work, but she was also consistently the one, gently and not so gently, reminding me that the deadlines were coming and I needed to peel myself off the couch or away from the guitar to get back to writing. Thank you, Saj. I love you.

Thanks to my kids, Maliyah and Tariq. You bring joy and energy to my life every single day. You inspire me not only to work hard but also to work in the pursuit of meaning and positive change. I love you endlessly.

Thank you to my parents, Keith and Marian Allingham, for their never-ending love and support, and for instilling in me a dogged and relentless work ethic.

Thank you to my friend and mentor Jeff Griffiths, who has supported me through the ups and downs of every single professional project I have ever taken on. He hired me at one of my first "real" jobs. He pushed me to work at the CBC. He designs my albums! Having that talented outside eye and ear to rely upon has been invaluable for many years now.

Thank you to my friend and CBC boss Shiral Tobin for supporting the *Major Misconduct* radio series from the start and for helping me navigate the licensing logistics with the CBC. She's a woman of her word!

The book publishing industry was a complete mystery to me before taking on this project. Thank you to my colleague and friend Grant Lawrence for talking and walking me through some of the ins and outs.

Thanks to the Society for International Hockey Research and, in particular, Taylor McKee, Kevin Slater, Michel Vigneault, and Len Gould. Your expertise helped make the history chapter sing.

Thank you to all of my teachers and professors of English and writing. I'd specifically like to acknowledge Doreen Ebbers and Lynie Tener, who truly taught me how to write.

Thank you to Samantha Haywood and Rob Firing at Transatlantic Agency. I feel like I've been in expert, steady hands on this book from the outset!

Thank you to Brian Lam, Robert Ballantyne, and everyone at Arsenal Pulp Press for championing this book and me as a new author. It means a lot.

JEREMY ALLINGHAM is an award-winning journalist and musician from Vancouver. He works for the CBC, where some of his most recent and poignant work has included in-depth coverage of fighting in junior hockey; the opioid crisis; climate catastrophe and the energy industry; local, provincial, and federal politics; the craft beer industry; and pretty much anything and everything sports and music related.